How to Start A Quality Childcare Business in Your Home

Everything You Need To Know

Melody Carlson

THOMAS NELSON PUBLISHERS
Nashville · Atlanta · London · Vancouver

This book is lovingly dedicated
to my husband, Christopher,
and sons Gabe and Luke.

Published in Nashville, Tennessee, by Thomas Nelson, Inc., Publishers, and distributed in Canada by Word Communications, Ltd., Richmond, British Columbia, and in the United Kingdom by Word (UK), Ltd., Milton Keynes, England.

Scripture quotations are from the NEW KING JAMES VERSION of the Bible. Copyright © 1979, 1980, 1982, Thomas Nelson, Inc., Publishers.

Library of Congress Cataloging-in-Publication Data

Carlson, Melody.
    How to start a quality childcare business in your home :
everything you need to know / Melody Carson.
        p.   cm.
    "Publishers, and distributed in Canada by Word Communications,
Ltd., Richmond, British Columbia."
    ISBN 0-7852-7969-5 (pbk.)
    1. Day care centers—Management.   2. Day care centers—Planning.
3. Small business—Management.   4. New business enterprises—
Management.   5. Creative activities and seat work.   I. Title.
HV851.C34   1995
362.7′12′068—dc20
                                                                                94–45498
                                                                                    CIP

Printed in the United States of America

2 3 4 5 6 7 — 01 00 99 98 97 96 95

Contents

Introduction

HAVE YOU, like thousands of other savvy moms, come to realize that working outside the home is not for everyone? Have you paused to weigh your paycheck against the costs of childcare, transportation, and wardrobe needs—not to mention juggling schedules for sick children—and wondered, is it really worth it? Or maybe you're a stay-at-home mom, but you find it difficult to make ends meet. Still, you're not ready to join the workforce because you don't want to miss those irreplaceable moments in your child's early years—first smiles, first steps, and lots of other firsts. You wonder how you can generate some extra income. Everyone knows it's hard to keep a family afloat, especially in today's economy. What is a mother to do?

What if someone offered you an "at home" job where you needed minimal, if any, special training? Where you could focus on your children, providing them with fun activities, new playmates, and wholesome meals, and still get your laundry done. You would work five-day weeks, no nights, no weekends, and you could even take an occasional day off. The wage could range from five to twenty dollars an hour. Sound too good to be true?

I am talking about a childcare business—in *your* home. No

I do not mean baby-sitting, like when you were sixteen and sat on the couch watching TV while the kids ran wild. I am referring to a childcare professional, the owner/operator of a vital business. Of course, it's not for everyone, but if you really like children and you're seeking a way to make money at home, it might be just what you're looking for.

Providing quality childcare has other rewards too. You make new friends and experience appreciation from other parents, who know their children are in good hands. You become an extended family to your customers, and your children have convenient playmates. You also have the opportunity to plant little seeds of God's truth in fresh young minds.

I want to show in a step-by-step format how to operate your own successful childcare business, starting from day one. I will cover everything from home safety to rainy day activities.

I have worked in almost every aspect of childcare: corporate care, on-site care, preschool, co-op care, group home care, and family childcare. It all adds up to nearly eighteen years of childcare expertise—including raising my own children (an experience you should never underestimate). Of all these various types of childcare experiences I have found family childcare, provided within the comfort of my home, to be my favorite. Not only that, but when it's provided in a professional manner, I don't think there's a better form of childcare available to parents who cannot be home with their little ones. Although I have my degree in early childhood education, it's not a prerequisite for providing quality family childcare.

Family childcare refers to caring for up to six children in your home. This type of care does not usually require state certification, but just the same, don't let regulations intimidate you. The following chapters will show how to create a childcare program that exceeds state standards. If this idea appeals to you, read along and discover the satisfaction of being home with your children and making money at the same time.

1

Beginnings:
What Makes a Good
Childcare Provider?

THAT DID IT! I was fed up with shoving my children out the door just to make it to work on time. And after work I would come home to dirty dishes piled in the sink, a mountain of smelly laundry, and "When's dinner?" I was ready to tumble off the working mom's merry-go-round. Yet I wondered how our family would fare without my extra (albeit meager) salary. There must be a better way.

I picked up the daily paper and frowned at the headlines. It appeared the proprietor of a local childcare business was being indicted on several counts of child abuse. The large center was reputed to have been a first-rate facility—and now this. How sad and frustrating for those parents.

I tossed down the paper and contemplated the plight of a society where young mothers get thrust from home to workplace just to survive today's economy. I ached for little ones evicted from their homes only to be warehoused in day care situations, sometimes for ten- to twelve-hour days. It all seemed hopelessly unfair. If there was one thing I could fix in this crazy world, it would be for children to be home with their mothers during those precious early years.

Fortunately for my family, I'd been able to stay home with

my boys when they were young, and then later, being a preschool teacher, I took them to work with me. But even as they became school age, I still wanted to be close by. I still wanted them to have someone to come home to.

Just then, it hit me. I *could* have it all! I could be home for my boys, I could make some extra money, *and* I could help other families in need of quality childcare. Right then and there I decided to look into the possibility of providing childcare as an in-home business. Although I had an extensive background in early childhood education, I knew relatively little about childcare as a home business. It sounded like the answer to a multitude of problems. As I investigated the prospects, I discovered few people offering what I would consider quality childcare in their homes. Many of those who did treated it more like baby-sitting. There was a missing ingredient—professionalism.

I called my state's Children's Services Division to request more information about in-home care, and then I read up on the current regulations for the two primary types of home care I was considering. Group home care is licensed care for up to twelve children, and family childcare can be offered with or without a license for up to six children (these ratios and license requirements vary slightly from state to state). Standards for group home care can be fairly stringent (such as requiring an early childhood degree and a large facility with separate bath-rooms). Therefore, this book focuses primarily on family child-care. However, everything in this book can be applied to group home care as well. In fact, I provided group home care for several years, but I must point out that caring for ten to twelve children is a very demanding job. On the other hand, I found family childcare to be much more low-key, comfortable, and compatible with raising a family.

I Want to Do This

How did I know this choice would be right for me? First, I felt certain it would help my family. But perhaps more important,

I knew I *wanted* to care for other children. Something stirred within me, and I really wanted to create a special place for children whose parents must work. This longing may have been a remnant from my own early childhood since my single mom worked full-time to support us. Consequently, my own care was sometimes less than desirable. My point is, I *wanted* to do this. From wherever the desire had sprung, it was there. And for me, the *wanting to* was the beginning.

So how about you? Are you looking for a way to make extra money, yet still be home with your children? You must be. Why else would you be reading this book? (Unless, of course, your mother-in-law gave it to you.) Which brings me to another point. Do not provide in-home care because a well-meaning friend, great-aunt Bessie, or even your dear sweet hubby thinks you should. You have to want it yourself. The desire must come from you.

Recently, I was talking with Debbie. She has provided family childcare for eleven years. Eleven years! I asked her how she got started and how she lasted so long.

"My kids were still little and I wanted to be home with them, plus I needed to earn some money," she said. "Besides that, I just wanted to do it. [You see, the desire was there.] And even after my children outgrew the need for childcare, I found I really enjoyed caring for children. I couldn't think of another job I'd rather be doing. By then my customers were more like family, and even as some children became school age, along came their younger siblings. I have never lacked for children, and I have even had to turn some away." Debbie explained, she may not do this forever, but for now she enjoys her work, and the money isn't bad either.

Counting the Cost

In the midst of making a decision like this, you must weigh the benefits against the drawbacks. You can do this by making a simple list of pros and cons. Place "Working at Home" on one side and "Working Outside the Home" on the other. For instance, on the "Working Outside the Home" column, consider things like childcare costs, travel time and expense, arrangements for a sick child, the stress of being on time, punching a time clock, pleasing a boss, and wardrobe expense (just think what you can save on pantyhose alone!). The downside of working at home might be no employee benefits, extra wear and tear on your home (tax deductible, though), and the additional responsibility of being your own boss.

Is This Job Right for You?

Before you apply for a new job, you need a basic understanding of the position. How else will you know if you are cut out for it? But just as it can be difficult to define the word *mother,* so it is with a *caregiver. Care* is a key word. Someone who cares about children is a good place to begin. From there you look for someone empathetic, who relates to little ones and actually enjoys their company, someone who appreciates their unique perspective. Are you the type of person who desires to nurture, to provide shelter, to create a safe refuge—a place where children feel at home? How do you respond to finger paint and crayons, Legos and Tinkertoys, scissors and paste?

There are many specific characteristics you expect to find in a good provider. You could probably list them: patience, compassion, understanding, tolerance, gentleness, and loving kindness. But you also need a fair amount of grit, self-discipline, perseverance, and perhaps most important, a good sense of humor.

So how do you know if *you* measure up? How can you predict whether you'd like to spend your days playing children's games, fixing snacks, sitting in pint-sized chairs, reading storybooks, and washing sticky little faces?

A "Childcare Provider's Aptitude Test" is at the end of this chapter. The results are not written in stone, and it is certainly no guarantee of success, but it might give you a general idea about whether you are cut out for this or not.

Do You Need Any Special Training?

Many skills and experiences could equip you to run a childcare business—from medical training to housekeeping to food services to personal banking. You do not need a college degree to provide quality care.

Perhaps the most precious expertise is what you have actually gained by parenting your own children. Never underestimate the significance of motherhood. Those endless hours spent mothering return a nice dividend in the area of childcare training. Even the best classroom instruction seldom replaces the reality of hands-on experience.

I hate to admit it, but before having my own kids, I was much less patient with other people's children. I loved the children, but I miscalculated that if I treated them in a certain way, they would respond likewise. Like one plus one equals two—right? Wrong. I had yet to appreciate that children are simply little people, and like their grown counterparts, they are individuals. Formulas do not necessarily work with them. For me, it took having my own children to fully comprehend this.

I am not suggesting that someone who has not had children will not make a good childcare provider. Some people are naturally gifted in this area. I just want to stress that motherhood makes an excellent teacher.

Two Final Essentials

Two basic personality traits make an excellent childcare provider. They are the two essential qualities I would seek if I needed someone to care for my own children.

I am talking about a positive attitude and healthy self-esteem. I know we have heard these catchphrases so frequently in the past couple of decades they have almost lost their meaning. But when we talk about caring for children, we need to take a fresh look.

A Positive Approach

It is indisputable. Children do better in a happy and positive atmosphere. If you praise a child for picking up his blocks, he'll work even harder next time. Positive words of encouragement motivate children like nothing else. Even while correcting a child you have a choice: you can either make it a positive learning experience, or a negative ordeal. Consider how you like to be dealt with—what motivates you toward excellence and achievement? Children are no different.

Self-Esteem

Self-esteem—what is it and where do we get it? Much of our self-esteem probably stems from our own early childhoods. Turn on any TV talk show and you'll see adults whose self-images were shattered as children, and, unfortunately, they're still trying to gather up the pieces.

Healthy self-esteem comes from seeing yourself as a valuable person with unique gifts and talents, created for a specific purpose. In other words, you like yourself. When you look in the mirror, can you smile and recognize you are a work of God? We all need to cultivate healthy self-esteem.

We should remember that having a positive view of ourselves is not the same as pride, nor is it an outcome of today's "me-first" pop psychology. It was Jesus who taught, "Love your neighbor as yourself." The connection here is so complete, so whole, it is almost inseparable. How can we love our neighbors if we don't love ourselves? What could create a better environment for young children than practicing this kind of love?

Childcare Is Not a "Last Chance" Option

Unfortunately these days, some people choose to provide childcare as a last option. They may think they cannot do anything else and surely anyone can watch kids. Too often they may already have a chip on their shoulder (not to mention low self-esteem), and it reflects in their attitude toward children. We do not need these people caring for our next generation. We, as a society, must return to valuing young children. We must recognize their early years as foundational to the rest of their lives.

Multitudes of young children are being cared for by unmotivated, barely educated, and sometimes even deviant caregivers. A large part of this problem stems from modern cultural roots because our society has devalued the young child—starting in the womb. Due to this misguided set of values, the care of the young is too often delegated to people who seem incapable of anything else. The childcare industry often recruits untrained workers who can be hired for minimum wage or less, people who come and go.

The childcare dilemma is recognized on the federal level, but government answers often involve state-controlled and tax-funded childcare centers. However, history and research have shown that children cared for in a stimulating, homey environment fair better than those who are institutionalized.

An Era of Hope

Lately, a new trend has begun, and it brings with it hope. An appreciation of family and family values has returned. Even folks in Hollywood are getting married and having babies these days, and this new focus on family might alter much of our nation's perspectives. Perhaps our society will once again learn to treasure young children and begin to view childcare with a new attitude. And this is where you, as a quality childcare provider, step in.

The Existing Need

Single mothers continue to abound, and our economy continues to oust a multitude of moms from home to join the labor force. The need for quality childcare is obviously here to stay. We hear statistics that claim as many as 50 percent of mothers work outside the home, and the baby boom continues. Therefore, in-home childcare provides two substantial options. First, it allows more moms to remain home with their children while contributing to the family income through childcare. Second, it furnishes more working moms with the pleasant alternative of nurturing and homey environments for their children.

The vast majority of early childhood experts agree that a child's personality and character are formed in the first few years of life. In that case, more than ever, we desperately need caring, intelligent, and capable providers to nurture our young children. We must realize that offering quality childcare is not merely a convenient means to make money at home; it's also a method to aid our culture. More than that, it's an opportunity to lovingly guide the next generation, to teach them the value of family and home. And if we're smart we'll plant some eternal seeds along the way.

So you see, childcare is much more than baby-sitting, and it is not something to jump into thoughtlessly. The following aptitude test can help you consider if this is really right for you, and the rest of this book will guide and encourage you through the basic steps of running a successful childcare business in your home.

Childcare Provider Aptitude Test

1 Do you like children (not just your own)? Do you enjoy their company and appreciate their spontaneity?

2 Are you easygoing? Can you wipe up spilled milk without shedding tears? Can you cope with noise?

3 Are you self-disciplined—a self-starter? Could you be your own boss?

4 Is your family supportive of this new employment opportunity? (Older children need to be considered too.)

5 Are you in pretty good physical shape, able to keep up with little legs that seldom slow down?

6 Can your home realistically contain a small childcare facility? (Fenced yard? Large open space? Good plumbing?)

7 Are you able to positively discipline children and get good results without resorting to punishment?

8 Do you take time for yourself? Do you nurture healthy self-esteem?

9 Would you leave your children with someone like you?

10 Have you asked God to guide you in this decision?

If you answer yes to most of these questions, you may have the right stuff!

2

I Think I Can, but What about the Rest of My Clan?

SO YOU'RE THINKING, *Maybe I do have the right stuff, but what about my family?* Without a doubt, you must consider the rest of your household. Do they have what it takes? An in-home business affects everyone under the roof, including Fido.

We chose to do some remodeling before I opened my childcare business. Consequently, my husband became totally involved in the process. He invested his own blood and sweat (I don't recall any tears) into creating a space to enhance our childcare business. I always called it "our" business. It was a joint venture, and I made a point to remind him. I could not have done it without him.

You may be an independent person, and you may be capable of swinging a mean hammer to repair that broken gate for the umpteenth time. But if you have a spouse, you need, at the very least, his nod of approval. You also want his respect for you as a businesswoman, which may require some informative communication on your part. You should let him know that you are not just baby-sitting and that you take childcare seriously—it is your job. You need his support. Is he ready for this type of commitment?

In the first chapter we considered your qualifications, but what about your spouse? Here are some questions to ask yourself and him: Does he have a tolerance for noise or the typical kind of controlled chaos that accompanies extra little feet and voices in your home? Is he willing to help with maintenance chores? (For safety reasons it's important to keep things in tip-top shape.) How will he react to the kid clutter that will likely accumulate in certain parts of your house and yard? Is he a lawn maniac? What if the children wear a path through the backyard? Is he a perfectionist? What if some budding Picasso tries out a crayon on the dining room wall?

On the more serious side, you must consider certain state regulations regarding any adults abiding in your home. To qualify for certification, you must fill out criminal history reports for you and your household. These reports will reveal any crimes committed against children (abuse, molestation, etc.). Any criminal history of this sort will disallow certification. Even if you don't seek licensed certification, you would be wise to reevaluate your direction in the area of childcare if there is any criminal history of this sort in your home. Even if the person has completed a counseling program and is fully recovered, it is probably not worth the risk. All it takes is one suspected incident (it does not even have to be real), and you'll be out of business and possibly facing criminal charges.

Another prerequisite for certification is having a tobacco and alcohol-free home during the hours of childcare. And of course, it must be drug-free at all times. That includes any visitors who might drop in. It's up to you to protect and maintain high standards in your childcare environment.

The Rest of the Gang

If you are a mom, you must also consider your own children. Are they willing and able to participate in this enterprise? You're in a great situation if your children are preschool age. You'll be importing playmates and new sources of entertainment, and your focus will be almost exclusively on their world. They can hardly help but benefit from your new business venture.

What about school-age children? How will they react? One advantage is they won't be farmed off to after-school care while you're at work, and they won't become latchkey kids. They will come home to you, and that's worth a lot. You can also enroll their energies as childcare helpers, which gives them a feeling of importance and necessity. Many children, these days, lack something that used to be taken for granted—*being needed.* At one time, children helped run farms, milk cows, and harvest crops. But today, many children feel unneccesary and even in the way.

In a home business you can delegate many jobs to your children that will lighten your load: sweeping, helping pick up, washing tables, taking out the trash, or vacuuming. I used to have a nightly checklist for my boys (they took turns cleaning up after the children left). They liked having it written down because they felt more independent at not having to be "told." Don't expect the jobs to be done perfectly at first (the *doing* is the important thing; perfection evolves slowly). Praise and encourage your children for trying their best. They often learn more by doing than being told how to do it "the right way."

Another way to employ your school-age children is to make them teacher's aides. Younger children love the attention of older ones. One of my boys used to play soccer coach with the preschoolers at recess time. Of course, they didn't get a real grasp on the game, but they sure had fun running back and forth and kicking the ball with all their might. You'll find that about the time your children come home, your energy level may be lagging, yet they're still ready to go.

Encourage your children's input and creativity. Consider what they are good at. If it's drama, how about puppetry or dress-up plays? If it's artistry, let them help direct a craft project. Are they learning to read? Invite them to read stories (little children are very patient with beginner readers). The possibilities are limitless, and the payoff is happy kids, both yours and those in your care.

What about teens? When providing care in a home inhabited by teens, you should ask these questions: Are your teens easygoing, helpful, and motivated? Can they support you in this new undertaking? Or will they resent sharing their home with, as they may refer to them, "babies"? Is there enough space in your home to maintain a separate area for your teens to feel comfortable after returning from school—at least their own bedrooms? Or can you work out a schedule so that sharing space will not be a problem?

Teens usually feel a need for their space, and if they haven't grown up with younger siblings, they may dislike this type of intrusion. If you are one of those fortunate parents blessed with responsible teens, you might hire them as relief workers. Naturally, you'll make certain to carefully train them and to clarify policies and procedures. You might even encourage your teens to take a first aid or Red Cross baby-sitting class. If your teens help care for children, you will want to make sure the parents are aware of that. Also give parents a chance to know your teens and be reassured their children are in good hands.

The many different jobs you may delegate to your children will help your business run smoothly. Your children will learn responsibility, and there'll be a sense of partnership between you and your children. They become actual stakeholders in the family business and in turn get to enjoy its success and benefits.

I kept a work log for my boys. They'd write in their amounts of time spent working and the dates. Then I would pay them weekly compensation for their labor. It was much more fulfilling than just doling out an allowance. They felt like they'd earned it, and I think they were more careful with how they spent it. Not only that, paying members of your family can become a tax deduction later. You are allotted a certain amount of deductions for household wages (money paid to members of your family who assist you in running a home business). Since tax laws change annually, check with your tax consultant for this amount. You might as well utilize this work deduction because the money goes back to your family in one way or another. Why not permit your daughter to purchase her Nikes with the deductible money she earned rather than pay taxes on that money and still have to buy her shoes anyway?

Childcare Rivalry

Another valid concern might be, "How will my children respond to sharing their mom—day in and day out?" This is a legitimate question. Young children, in particular, can be very possessive of their parents. Handled carefully and honestly, this problem can be minimized for both you and your children. It can also afford you the opportunity to reinforce to your own children how important they are, how much you love them, and how you appreciate their willingness to share their home and family.

When you provide full-time childcare it's imperative to ensure each child's space in your home. She needs a place where she can escape the throng, usually her own bedroom (one good reason not to make a child's room into a group play area). There will also be times you will need her to go to her room for disciplinary measures. Rest assured, your child will probably test you more than the rest. After all, they are on *her* turf. Unfortunately, you cannot safely furnish that type of refuge to other children in your care. Since you are their supervisor, they should remain in areas where you can hear or observe them throughout the day.

Another strategy to keep your older kids from singing the "childcare-in-my-home blues" is to adjust your schedule so that when they come home, you won't be too busy to hear about their day. I used to hire a preteen neighbor girl to help out with the children after school, which freed up my time a little. I stayed close by (within earshot) while she helped supervise the children waking up from naps, putting on shoes, and getting ready for a snack. This gave me a break, plus the chance to touch base with my boys.

Some children become unreasonably demanding simply because they see that Mom is engaged with another child. It's that little green-eyed monster called jealousy. But if you make yourself available to your children on a regular basis, you will likely notice that the demand situation will lighten up considerably. In fact, when your children realize you really are available, they might just toss you a "Hi, Mom" and be off on their merry way.

The flip side to the "sharing Mom" question is: How do *you* feel about sharing your children's time with others? Are you able to show equal attention to other children in your home without feeling that you have stolen something from your own children? Can you remain a fair and impartial referee in a dispute that involves your little angels? Will the other children in your home detect favoritism and feel like second-class citizens? You must comprehend how damaging that would be to a child staying in someone else's home. Try to mentally put yourself (or your children) in those shoes. Remember the stories about "wicked stepmothers." You certainly don't want to be cast in that role. Children have a great sense of fairness. They quickly notice inequality, especially if it is directed toward them. When you care for others' children, no one expects you to love them as much as your own, but the appearance should be so. What is truly amazing is how you can adopt these children into your heart. They can become almost like your own, and they will know you love them.

United We Stand

To succeed, you'll need your family's backing in this endeavor. You need solidarity. Otherwise having a home childcare business could stress your marriage beyond imagination. It could possibly place your whole family at risk. But if family members can unite energies toward this purpose, it could be the making of your family. It could reveal and develop strengths and talents they never knew existed. It could give your family a sense of a cooperative mission, and it could pass down to your children the legacy of the value of working together to achieve a common goal. Providing family childcare is, as the term implies, a family enterprise, and it takes the whole crew to keep the ship afloat.

3

Your Home:

Can It House a

Childcare Business?

Sizing Up Your Space

Most people cannot reconstruct their homes to accommodate a childcare facility, and besides, part of the charm of family childcare is the homey environment you won't find in a large day care facility. Just the same, you should evaluate whether or not your home can adapt to the needs of more little bodies. And if so, how many little bodies?

Most states require a facility to have at least thirty-five square feet of floor space per child. Even if you're not seeking state certification, this is a reliable figure to work around. Thirty-five square feet per child may sound like a lot at first, but consider that an average family room has around two hundred square feet (enough to accommodate about six children). Add in the other spaces you will use (bathroom, kitchen, and such), and you will find it's truly a minimal standard and not hard to meet. It is also a comfortable guideline for the number of children you would want to have in your home. It's no fun to pack them in like sardines.

The Lay of the Land

The floor plan of your home is essential to consider as well. Sometimes it helps to draw a rough blueprint of your house. You may want to switch some areas. One woman who had decided to do childcare had a seldom used dining room off her kitchen. She temporarily stored her traditional dining room furnishings and turned this spacious and light room into a main play area. I'm sure someday, when her children are older and she no longer provides care, she'll transform it back into a dining room again. So if your home seems limited, let your mind be creative. Otherwise you might overlook a nifty alternative. Remind yourself, this is not a lifetime commitment. Some people do childcare for only a few years while their own children are young.

A high priority in your floor plan is an easily accessible bathroom (located close to your primary play area). It isn't practical, or safe, to have the bathroom situated at one end of your house when you must supervise children at the other end. Children use the bathroom frequently and often require your assistance. If you're concerned about an out-of-the-way bathroom, consider whether it is at least within hearing distance. If it is, you may be okay.

Your kitchen should be handy too, although its location is easier to work around if you prepare meals and snacks ahead of time. As you scrutinize your kitchen, try to determine whether it is child friendly (safe) or not. If it isn't, can the entrance be gated or barricaded? Also consider where you will want children to eat. Spills are a regular part of childcare and a scrubbable floor is almost essential. You can, however, use a large section of oil cloth (fabric-backed vinyl) under the eating or craft area if wall-to-wall carpeting is an obstacle.

Decide which entrance the parents will use to deliver and pick up their children. You will probably want it near the main play area (unless you don't mind parents trekking through your home). Is there a handy spot to place a small wall unit or cubby shelf to store children's coats and gear?

How will children get to and from an outside play yard? Do you have a corner to stash those dirty shoes and boots? It's convenient if your outdoor exit isn't too far removed from the bathroom, because it never seems to fail—as soon as you get them bundled up and outside, someone needs to go potty.

The Look of the Land

Often it is hard for us to objectively view our homes. After all, we see them daily and can almost become blind to certain things. For a change, envision your home the way another parent might see it (and while you are at it, pretend it is an extremely overprotective parent). Look around your house. Is it clutter free? Could it be? Children need open spaces to roam and play. Do you have easily movable furnishings that could be rearranged to make the main play area more open and spacious? Could you get rid of some things to provide more floor space? Maybe it is time for a garage sale anyway. (They say the Spartan look is becoming quite in vogue these days. You might end up on the cutting edge of interior design.) Whatever it takes, create a space that invites children to move freely and play safely.

On the aesthetic side, is your overall home environment pleasant? Does it appear cheerful, friendly, fresh, and clean? These are some of the first things parents notice. Erroneous as it may be, in most cases parents tend to judge childcare by its packaging. Many large corporate childcare businesses have found cute trappings can really pull parents in. Although it's a good marketing technique, it does not guarantee good care. But what parent would want to leave a child in a dumpy-looking place? The fact is, most parents already feel guilty for leaving their children at all, but if the place at least looks good, they may be somewhat reassured. Unfortunately, many parents are forced to compromise even those minimal standards for lack of good childcare options, but that's where you come in. So don't forget to evaluate your packaging.

Some of your customers may already know and trust you. They may gladly overlook any housekeeping shortcomings just because they are so happy to have you look after their children.

But as a businesswoman, you'll want to come across as professional and capable. Your home helps reflect this image of efficiency. It will also assist you in earning parental respect and appreciation. When parents view you as something much more than a baby-sitter, they're more likely to make prompt childcare payments and pick up their children on time (and believe me, that's worth a lot when 5:30 rolls around and you're tired). A home that looks neat is another way to show you take your job seriously, and consequently, parents will take you seriously.

Some Basics

You will also need to determine whether your home has adequate heating, lighting, and proper ventilation. Naturally, different climates will dictate these needs. Where I live (in the Pacific Northwest) it can be very humid on a wet day, and that humidity multiplies with a bunch of moist little bodies in the room. I often used a ceiling fan as well as an air vent. You need fresh air sources, preferably screened windows that open easily. If your room is not on ground level, you need windows above child height or some protective device to keep children from falling out. A screen will not prevent a fall and may even encourage a fall if a child leans against it.

The ideal room for children would be light and airy on ground level with plenty of windows. Of course, not every home has lots of windows, but with good lighting and some bright and cheerful pictures on the wall, you can create a similar atmosphere.

With lighting, remember that floor lamps and children do not mix well. Light fixtures with bare bulbs or fluorescent tubes are potentially dangerous, especially if an object (like an airborne block) should strike. If lighting seems inadequate, you might consider wall lights (portable lamps that can be securely attached to the wall and plugged into an electrical outlet). This provides instant light without the threat of getting knocked over.

Temperature control is another important factor. You need a system that can maintain and regulate a constant temperature around seventy degrees, preferably year-round. Naturally, unless you have air-conditioning, this may be difficult in the heat of summer, but as long as you use fans and ventilation, anything under eighty degrees should be tolerable (remember that fans should be placed out of reach of children). With any heating system, you need to consider potential burns. The safest system will always be forced air. If your home is warmed by another source, you must determine its safety. Obviously, woodstoves, fireplaces, and even baseboard heaters can cause a child to get burned if used in a play area. Such heat sources must be securely barricaded. Some types of 220 volt electrical wall heaters (such as baseboard) can be replaced with thermostat-controlled fan heaters, which are safer for children.

Speaking of Safety

Safety is the primary consideration in determining whether your home is a good candidate for childcare. Stairs are potentially dangerous unless they can be blocked with a safety gate to prevent access to children. A brick fireplace hearth can leave quite a lump if a child stumbles, but you can create a foam pad to soften the corners. Often there are ways to reduce safety hazards without dismantling your entire home.

One hint in childproofing is to get down on a child's level. Actually crawl around and see what a child sees. Suddenly, you will notice things like exposed electrical outlets, tippy tables, electrical cords, or tall (climbable?) bookshelves not secured to the wall. Other things to look for might include the following:

- Kitchen stove: child-accessible knobs, hot oven door
- Dangerous kitchen appliances, including trash compactor, garbage disposal, and blender. (A running dishwasher

opened during a cycle can scald a child. Any electrical appliance requires supervision.)

- Slippery floors, especially if wet
- No hand railings on stairs with more than two steps
- Spindles on railings (Child's head might wedge between spindle spaces wider than about four inches.)
- Area rugs that slide (Get webbed rubber mats to hold them in place.)
- Poisonous indoor plants
- Water heater too hot (Tap water can scald a child.)
- Any cleaning solvents or poisonous chemicals stored within reach of children (Use safety latches and high shelves.)
- Any medications stored within reach of children
- Doors that swing too easily (smashed fingers)
- Uncovered electrical outlets (Plug holes with safety covers.)
- Loose cords (tripping hazard)
- Extension cords (fire hazard)
- Unsafe rockers or recliners (pinched fingers)
- Garbage cans (lidded, stored away from play area)
- Exposed light bulbs or fluorescent tubes (shattered glass)
- Firearms (They must be locked up and stored away from children.)

It's impossible to list every potential safety problem. The key is to use common sense when evaluating your home. If you see hazards, try to determine how they can be minimized or eliminated.

Small Sacrifices

An undeniable inconvenience in using your home for a childcare business is that you must look at it differently. It is no longer just your home. Occasionally, you must sacrifice some aesthetics to be practical and safe. Before you take the plunge, decide if it is worth it. If you have small children, you have nothing to lose by childproofing your home. In fact, you may actually prevent a serious accident for one of your own.

I heard someone say, "Every room should have some items that are off-limits to children in order to teach the meaning of no." I don't agree, especially in the case of full-time childcare. Believe me, there are plenty of times to tell children no. Why not eliminate all you can? It's not difficult to see that antiques, breakables, delicate upholstery, and multitudes of plants do not mix with small children. Besides the prospect of costly damage, you do not want to repeat all day long, "Hands off. Don't touch that! No, no, no!"

Childcare Decor

I am not suggesting you strip your home bare. I love to decorate, and it would have been difficult for me to have administered cheerful care in a stark and boring room. But I did remove most of the plants and antiques and all of the breakables. I then adjusted my decor (in the childcare room) to accommodate the needs of young children, yet not neglecting to please my own eye. I started out by selecting a couple of my favorite colors (cranberry red and hunter green) and a country theme (popular at the time). Using paint, fabrics, and ingenuity, I decked the room with stenciled hearts and checkerboards, teddy bear wreaths, and bright tartan plaids. Of course, there were plenty of toys, and I stored them in sturdy red plastic crates and boxes. I maintained the red-and-green theme in cups and dishes, chairs and cots—everything.

My decorating gave what could have seemed like a cluttered and busy room (with all that kid stuff) nice continuity. It was quite a pleasant room, and the grown-ups appreciated it as much as the children did. Not only that, it was a room my family felt comfortable in (good thing, since it was also our family room). But even as my boys grew older, they did not mind sharing the room with childcare, because it was not a bit babyish.

So you do not have to resort to blue bunnies and pink kitties (unless you like them) to create a child-pleasing environment. It is also a well-researched fact that young children respond to and are intellectually stimulated by vivid colors. That is why we see so many developmental learning toys in the primary colors: red, yellow, and blue. You could pick any combination of two or three bright colors and create a fun room the whole family can enjoy. You could do a modern theme with bold blocks of red and yellow or a southwestern theme with bright turquoise and coral. The options are only as limited as your imagination.

Mapping It All Out

Now that you have mentally started to redecorate your kid space, you might also start figuring where you could carve some niches for separating various activities. Make some rough drafts of your house so you can play with the spaces and estimate how many children you can plan to accommodate.

Determine where a resting area might be and how you could arrange cots or mats. Where might you position a low table for crafts and an eating area? Another important area will be the quiet corner, a place where children can snuggle up with a book or a teddy bear. Or how about a construction corner where you can keep noisy blocks and building toys? (A carpeted area is quieter and easier on ears.) Where can you place some storage shelves? Portable shelves with backs that can be reversed against the wall (to hide toys and stuff) will prevent your home from looking like Kiddie Kingdom seven days a week. After all, it's still your home, and you want to live there comfortably without the constant reminders of your childcare business.

Before I actually started my business, I sketched the layout of my room to half-inch equals one foot scale, along with half-inch-scale furniture pieces (cut out of paper) like resting cots, tables, and chairs. I played house on paper by moving the pieces around to make sure that the space would work and that everything (including the children) would fit.

The Great Outdoors

Now you've considered your home's interior, but what about the exterior? Children need to be outdoors, and a good childcare facility accommodates that need. A cautious parent will examine your outside play areas just as closely as the inside, and as a professional, you'll want a first-rate play yard. That does not necessarily mean expense, but it does mean safety. First of all you need a fenced area. The fence does not have to be tall, or even private. It just needs to be sturdy, secure, and at least three feet tall.

While in college, I worked at a center that temporarily removed their existing fence to replace it with a new one. The children had always played right up to the fence line before, often climbing on the fence to see over. But they clustered in the middle of the play yard, afraid to venture as far as they normally would when the fence was up. It was interesting to note how a simple thing like a fence gave them such a sense of security. It shows how much children need boundaries. And for your peace of mind, not to mention their safety, so do you.

The play yard should have a soft, well-drained play surface. Young children tend to tumble a lot. In drier climates grass is ideal, but where I live, we used a separate area with a generous coating of sawdust for the wet season (the grass gets too muddy). Unfortunately, the sawdust adhered to some clothing, but we kept a whisk broom handy, and the children took turns brushing each other off.

As you appraise your yard's potential, consider how easy it might be to supervise a handful of children playing in it. Are there hidden corners or excessive shrubbery that would obstruct your view? A safe yard will be clean and clutter free. Watch out for and eliminate these and any other backyard hazards:

- Old appliances, freezers, refrigerators, etc. (can trap and suffocate children)
- Uncovered wood piles (can tumble if climbed upon)
- Accessible tools (falls and cuts)
- Any water source—pool, pond, well (drowning)
- Any low electrical wires (could be touched with a stick)
- Poisonous plants (such as laurel, rhododendron, ornamental berries)
- Unlocked sheds or outbuildings
- Power equipment within reach of children (mowers, etc.)
- Debris, garbage, or boards with nails
- Tempting dangers (If there are unsafe yet climbable trees, remove lower limbs.)
- Vegetation with thorns
- Slick surfaces, like wooden decks (no running)

Again, every yard is unique. Use your head as you evaluate yours. If necessary, ask another (more objective) observer if she notices any potential threats to safety.

Everyone faces some hurdles in analyzing the home's adaptability to childcare. But as long as you keep safety foremost, other less crucial obstacles should be surmountable. Also remember an advantage to providing family childcare (in most states) is that you do not have to comply with any overly rigid regulations regarding your home. But if you follow the advice in this book, you should meet and exceed most of these requirements anyway. Add your integrity and good sense, and you have a foolproof formula for success.

Basic Considerations about Your Home for Childcare:

1 Space minimum standard: thirty-five square feet per child

2 Safety obstacles: woodstove, stairways, etc.

3 Easy-to-use floor plan (play area, bathroom access, etc.)

4 Utilities (good heating, lighting, plumbing, etc.)

Ways to Develop Your Home for Childcare:

1 Make a blueprint (lay out the childcare areas).

2 Unclutter your home (garage sale time).

3 Perk up the face of your home (welcoming front porch/entry).

4 Create a friendly interior (a place where both children and parents will feel at home).

5 Deal with safety problems (safety gates, nonslip rugs, etc.).

4

Starting Out:

The Basics

INVENTORY NEEDS VARY from home to home, but two primary factors help determine your basic requirements: (1) the number of children you intend to care for, and (2) the age group. By knowing how many children you will care for, you can estimate how much equipment you will need. Deciding which age group determines the type of equipment you need, such as cribs or cots, high chairs or low chairs. Since the needs of infants vary so much from those of preschoolers, we will consider baby supplies in the following chapter. But whether we choose to care for one baby or six toddlers, we all start from the same place; we must take stock of what we already have and then conclude what we need to provide quality care. You do this by making a two-column list with "Have" on one side and "Need" on the other.

If you have young children, you will also likely possess an assortment of the smaller things like games, toys, and books. Although that is an excellent start, and you want to list those on the "Have" side, you may not have enough to occupy up to six children, or you many not have as many educational toys as you would like. We will address some inexpensive and creative options for acquiring a better inventory of those things in Chapter 6. But before that, we need to consider what you require in the area of large furnishings.

Tables and Chairs

I do not know what I would have done without my little red stackable chairs and two big tables. I ordered them from a preschool supply catalog, and I never regretted the initial investment (about twenty dollars a chair, sixty dollars a table). We used those tables and chairs for everything: crafts, snacks, games, puzzles, sharing time, meals, or whatever. The children could easily maneuver and transport the lightweight, yet durable, chairs, and the low, round tables were sturdy enough to dance a jig on, though we never actually tried it.

Of course, there are other options for kid seating, from homemade wooden benches to molded plastic outdoor chairs. But these are the questions you should ask: Are they sturdy and lightweight? Do they tip easily? Are they safe? Can they be stored easily to provide more play space? (On foul weather days it's nice to open up as much area as possible for large-muscle activities such as controlled hopping, skipping, and jumping.)

As for tables, how wide, how tall, and how many? It depends on the amount of floor space and the number of children, but it is best to have enough table room for all children to be seated at once. Round tables are nice because you eliminate corners for bumping (and tables are usually around shin height—your shins, that is). Whichever type tables you choose, they should be sturdy, nontippable, and topped with a nonporous scrubbable surface, like plastic laminate. The round tables I used were adjustable height and sixty inches wide (big enough to seat six children comfortably). My family often used those tables when the children were not around. They were handy for various projects; we even used them for a wedding reception once. Eventually, when I ceased doing childcare, I sold all my inventory to a friend who was just starting out (returning some of my initial investment), but we still miss those tables at times.

Naptime Needs

Another necessity for full-time care is a resting place for each child. I used conventional preschool-sized stacking cots with aluminum frames and washable canvas coverings (cheaper when purchased by sets of six from supply catalogs). They come in toddler size, preschool size, and a larger size for older children. They can be stacked and stored in a closet. Again, it is an initial investment (about twenty dollars per cot), but it was worth it to me. Foldable resting mats are also available.

Another slightly less expensive option is to make your own resting mats by covering two-inch-thick, child-sized foam pads with a waterproof casing. You need basic sewing skills, and it helps to have a do-it-yourself upholstery outlet where they cut foam to order (about twenty-four inches by fifty-four inches). Then cut your waterproof covering (two sides, about twenty-six inches by fifty-six inches), place outside in, and stitch a one-half-inch seam like a pillowcase (leaving one end open). Turn outside back out and insert the foam pad; then stitch the open end.

A mat or cot should be individually labeled for each child and covered by washable cotton sheets (to be changed regularly, with spares on hand). Sheets are also easy to make. Cut fabric rectangles several inches larger than cots or mats, and then shirttail hem all the edges. You can either gather corners with elastic or (for cots) attach six-inch tabs with Velcro on corners that can be wrapped and secured around cot legs.

I encouraged children to provide their own familiar blankets from home. I remember one mother of twins, who made special quilts for her daughters. Not only was their bedding cute and snuggly, but it gave the girls something to look forward to on their first day at the childcare center. I also kept some spare "blankies" around. I made them by cutting a queen-sized thermal blanket into quarters and binding the edges.

Some people who provide homecare choose to offer their family members' beds and bedrooms for naptime, but I don't recommend this practice if you can avoid it. Children really appreciate having their own cot and designated resting spot. And you maintain an element of security by keeping everyone within view of everyone else. Besides, most parents will not like the idea of children secluded in bedrooms. If you're worried that children will not sleep in groups, I can guarantee from experience that if they have enjoyed a full and active day and are then provided with a quiet darkened room, they most often *will* go to sleep. It really does not matter that other resters are in close proximity. Just make sure they're a good arm's length away from each other.

A Place for All Their Stuff

It is inevitable. Jill arrives in the morning with boots, a book to share, her blankie, a jacket, and who knows what else. By five o'clock she has accumulated two paintings, a craft project, and some interesting leaves to add to her stuff. Where do you put it all? Most childcare centers use what are affectionately referred to as cubbyholes. Basically they are vertical open shelves where a child can hang her coat and keep spare clothes, blankets, toys, or whatever. But it is the child's own space—to share with no one. These shelves are relatively simple to construct (see diagram at end of chapter) and, I think, well worth the initial expense.

Another option is to place, close to the entry, coat hooks mounted on a removable board (see diagram; big round cabinet knobs are safer than hooks). Below each coat "hook" you can keep a plastic bucket or crate marked with each child's name. It isn't a lot of space, but it will help keep their stuff together. Then you can stash hooks and buckets out of sight when you want to magically transform your childcare center back into a home. However you cope, you must anticipate the stuff that will accompany each child.

If your space is really limited, you might ask parents to provide a carryall bag (like a nylon gym sack) marked with the child's name. Then the child's coat and things can be zipped inside and tossed into a spare room. Of course, the children will need to get to their bags throughout the day.

Labeling

With all these things to keep separate, you'll soon see the need for labeling. But you ask, "What if children cannot recognize their names?" A couple of solutions can help the children learn to recognize their names. One is to use a specific color for each child. Use multicolored construction paper blocks, a different color for each child with their names clearly printed (purple for Krissy, blue for John, and so on). Repeat the same color/name combination throughout (cubbies, cots, etc.). These labels can be laminated by covering with clear Con-Tact paper. (Clear Con-Tact paper also comes in handy for protective coverings on game boards, books, homemade card games, and such.) Another option is to use picture stickers next to each child's name (remember those little sticker booklets with repetitive pages?). The children can easily learn to recognize Becky as the bunny or Brett as the racoon. Again, repeat the same animal throughout, so the child is not confused. These, too, can be laminated.

Other Furnishings

Some other large pieces you may need could be bookshelves, storage shelves, storage crates, and a file cabinet. These needs will be determined according to your space and your circumstances. There are other storage options too. Don't overlook things like plastic (milk) crates, large woven baskets, plastic laundry baskets, or mesh laundry bags. These can be used for storing toys, games, books, and other kid stuff.

Often it's difficult to decide exactly what you will need in the way of extras until you actually provide care. I found some things to be unnecessary and even in the way. It's usually better to start out sparsely rather than to overload your childcare space with too much junk. Remember, kids need opportunities to exercise their creativity. If you go out and find a fully equipped child-sized kitchenette, how will children learn to improvise, to turn a stool into a stove or a crate into a refrigerator? More is not always better.

What I Really Need List

1 Make a "Have List" of things you already have (bookshelf, child-sized rocking chair, cassette tape player, etc.).

2 Make a "Need List" of things you feel certain you must have to provide quality care (tables, chairs, storage, mats, etc.).

3 Prioritize the "Need List." What do you absolutely need to provide quality care?

4 Work out your budget. How much do you have? How much will it cost?

5 Start checking out garage sales (but stick to your list).

6 Get a good preschool/childcare supply catalog.

7 Decide to use your creativity (think of other uses of things, such as making a giant cable spool into an outdoor play toy).

MOVABLE COAT HANGER

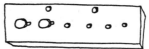

ATTACH ROUND CABINET KNOBS
THROUGH HOLES DRILLED 6" APART ON
1"x6" BOARD CUT TO APPROPRIATE LENGTH
—DRILL 2 HOLES ON TOP TO HANG UP

"CUBBY HOLE" STORAGE

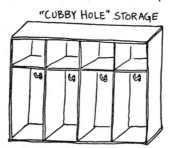

CUBBIES SHOULD BE ABOUT 36" TALL
EACH ABOUT 12" WIDE X 12" DEEP
MADE OF PLYWOOD (PAINTED) WITH
COAT HOOK IN BACK

5

Caring for

Babies and

Toddlers

ADDRESSING THE CHILDCARE needs of babies is difficult for me—partly because I question whether group care is in the best interest of such young children, and partly because I think so few people are truly capable of providing quality care for more than one or two infants at the same time. The fact is, like it or not, the need for quality infant care is a reality in today's society. Multitudes of mothers return to the workforce within weeks of delivery. Therefore, my hat is off to people who earnestly desire to offer qualified and loving care to infants.

Most states require a ratio of not more than four infants (under twelve months old) to one care giver. Although some states allow more, I think four-to-one is a relatively safe guideline. I know from personal experience that I wouldn't want to care for more than four babies. It can be a real nightmare! So, you wonder, what happened? What was my nightmare? I cannot resist sharing this story simply because it is, to this day, rather unbelievable.

About twenty years ago, I was fresh out of college. With my early child ed degree in hand, I had just arrived overseas to teach preschool on a large mission base in the South Pacific. Before my already designated job began (teaching the five-year-old class), I was assigned to the baby nursery in order to allow the regular caregiver a two-week holiday. It also happened to be the beginning of a two-week translation conference, and translation workers came to the base from all over (and with them, their children). The nursery normally accommodated six to eight babies, and there was also a helper (a local woman who barely spoke English). That morning I greeted the first mother, and confidently took her frightened child and soothed him.

Soon more babies arrived, and things grew busier, with consequently less time for soothing. They just kept coming, one after the other. More and more babies. It was like when the Cat in the Hat kept pulling more cats out of his hat; only it was babies—about twenty of them! And all in that tiny nursery. It would have been illegal in the States. The helper and I dashed to and fro, trying to meet the needs of all the screaming babies without stepping on them. We had an assembly line for diaper changes, and in the closet-sized bathroom three or four potty-chairs were constantly in use. I will never forget one toddler, Murray—a big boy, with a big smile, and one of the few who was not crying. In the midst of all the mayhem, dear little Murray decided to empty all the potty-chairs—right onto the bathroom floor. What a smell!

Now when I look back, I think that regular nursery worker knew exactly what she was doing by taking her holiday during conference time. I honestly do not know how I survived those two weeks, except that I was young and God is gracious. Since that experience, I have steered away from providing childcare to babies. But it does give me a healthy respect for the four-to-one ratio.

The Basic Equipment

Caring for babies and toddlers is a lot different from caring for preschoolers. For one thing, babies seem to require so much more gear than preschoolers, and yet even that can be kept to a minimum. First, you must consider their basic needs: food, sleep, changing, holding, and some entertainment. With babies, unlike preschoolers, it is not necessary for all of them to eat at the same time. So one high chair per child is not necessary, but you may need a couple. Choose a high chair with a t-strap safety belt to prevent sliding and a secure detachable tray that can be washed easily. As with all furnishings for young children, check the high chair for sharp edges, splintering, sturdiness, and stability. Convenience in storing may be a factor if your space is limited, but most high chairs fold down.

Some parents like to provide the baby's own infant seat, but you may want a spare one on hand as well. An infant seat needs a t-strap safety belt, too, and should be used only according to the manufacturer's instructions. A baby swing can often soothe an unhappy baby, but it is no replacement for being held and rocked. A comfortable rocker is almost a necessity, but rocker rungs can present a hazard to babies crawling on the floor.

A diaper-changing table is essential. It should be a comfortable height for you and topped with a vinyl-covered changing pad. There should be enough room to place both baby and diaper bag. A shelf above the table can provide more storage space. The changing area should be equipped with disposable wipes, toilet paper, spare disposable diapers (just in case the parent forgets), Vaseline for diaper rash (use medicated ointments only with a written parental request), baby powder (to be used only as needed and with caution; the baby should not inhale it), disinfectant spray (out of the the baby's reach, of course), paper towels, and a covered wastebasket (emptied regularly). This is also a good place to locate emergency medical supplies: nasal aspirator, rectal thermometer, Band-Aids, and so forth.

Thank goodness, babies do sleep. You may need one crib per baby. Portable cribs use less space than conventional cribs, and there are small stackable cribs designed specifically for group care (although they look a bit like cages). Cribs should be sturdy, the mattress should fit snugly, and the spindles should be less than three inches apart. When infants are very young, they can nap in infant seats or mobile beds (these can be provided by parents), but that won't last long because babies grow fast. Crib mattresses must be waterproof, and there should be plenty of fresh sheets ready for quick changes. Bumper pads, though cute, are not necessary, and they can even be dangerous, especially if they have string ties. You really need only a clean sheet and a soft baby blanket.

If you choose to use walkers, jumpers, or any other baby furniture accessories, make certain they are safe. Some parents may want to provide their own. It may be cheap and easy to pick up these items at garage sales and secondhand stores, but they won't come with the manufacturers' instructions or information about any potential safety hazards or recalls. So before you buy, evaluate. Use the basic safety questions: Is it sturdy? Are there any sharp or jagged edges? Can it tip? Are there any small movable parts that could be dislodged or ingested? Can it be cleaned easily? If you are unsure, do not buy it. It isn't worth the risk.

I remember a cute circular-design walker that was very popular when my children were babies. Unfortunately, we soon found its attractive circular design also allowed it to tip easily when transferring from hard floor to carpet. It is hard enough to see your own little darling dumped on his noggin because you have accidentally made a poor choice of baby equipment, but this is definitely not a discovery you want to make with someone else's child.

Some Big Necessities

There are some items you should not be without when you provide care for infants. If I was the mother of a baby looking for quality childcare, I would expect you to have them. First of all, you absolutely must have a good refrigerator that maintains a steady temperature of thirty-five degrees in order to keep food fresh and wholesome. You also need proper laundry facilities. The only way to get around this would be to keep a large quantity of baby bedding and go to the Laundromat daily. Next, nothing sanitizes like a dishwasher. It's quick and convenient, and it allows you more time to nurture those little ones, although an option would be to use disposable utensils and dishes. The last, but not least, item is a microwave. It can be a small, inexpensive one because you need it only for warming. But when you have more than one baby in the house, a microwave can be a real lifesaver when eating time rolls around. (Just make sure to test the temperature of food or formula in case it is too hot.)

Health and Nutrition

If I planned to offer care for babies and toddlers, my first contact would be the state Children's Services Division to request information on the minimal group care standards for this age group. These regulations vary from state to state, and they are constantly changing and being upgraded, but they give you some very definite guidelines in regard to health, sanitation, nutrition, record keeping, and such.

Many states require certified centers to record all nutritional intake with infants, down to the last ounce and the time it was consumed. This is a good practice to keep parents informed of their child's eating habits, plus you will know exactly when Susie had her last bottle. Some parents will want to provide their child's food. If you plan to reuse leftover portions of formula or baby food, clearly label it with the child's name, seal in a plastic bag, and refrigerate promptly, and only do this one time per item. It's also advisable to thoroughly wash bottle nipples before refrigerating a partially used bottle. Certification standards in some states may even prohibit the reuse of uneaten portions. This may seem wasteful, but it is for health and sanitation reasons. Opened portions of food stored improperly can make children seriously ill. Always make certain any bottles, dishes, or utensils are sanitized through a dishwasher or sanitizing solution between use. (Chapter 12, "An Ounce of Prevention," provides further information on sanitation procedures in caring for babies.)

Here are a couple of things to keep in mind should you choose to care primarily for babies and toddlers: What will your age cap be, and will it be difficult to part ways when those sweet little cherubs outgrow your facility? Of course, some people love caring exclusively for these little ones, and any parent should be thankful to find such a childcare situation. Also remember, childcare fees always run much higher for babies and toddlers than with preschoolers; this is nice, since your ratio also decreases with this age group. Research the market by phoning around your area to come up with the going rate and don't apologize for higher rates. Babies and toddlers definitely require a higher level of care—it should cost more!

6

Now for the
Fun Stuff

NOW THAT WE have examined the larger furnishing needs of a childcare center, we can focus on the fun stuff—you know, the toys, games, and art supplies. You need a plan, and it's time to make lists again. Remember those two columns: what you have and what you need. You can simplify things by deciding what sort of a center you wish to create.

Most good childcare facilities are divided into what are called learning centers. These are separate areas for different types of activities, such as a block corner or a book section. You can start by looking at your room and figuring where to set up active areas and where to keep quiet areas (remember that blueprint in chapter 3). Now you can even break it down further into specific interest areas, and that will help you organize the items you may still need. Following are some suggestions, but you may have other ideas you wish to implement, depending on the type of care you will be facilitating.

Quiet Corner

A quiet corner is a special place for a child to curl up with a picture book or teddy bear. In the busyness of group childcare, children especially need their quiet moments. Can't you, even as an adult, relate? Yet often, as a caregiver, you must foster and, at times, impose quiet moments for a child who is on the verge of losing control. (I call this preventive discipline and we'll discuss it more later.)

The minimal requirements for this area are a carpet or an oversized pillow or beanbag chair, some books, and a couple of stuffed toys. If you already have a sofa in your playroom, it might provide a comfortable location for your quiet corner, especially if your floor space is in demand. You could add some big soft pillows to make the sofa more cozy. Fake fur makes wonderful coverings for kid pillows and can even be sewn into animal shapes. If your sofa shows wear and tear, you might throw a soft blanket over it while the children are about.

This is the ideal place for keeping books available. Books need not be expensive to please children. I have seen Little Golden Books (purchased for a dime each at a garage sale) entertain children again and again. Little hands appreciate small maneuverable books they can easily hold and read. Large picture books are great for group reading, and the public library is an inexpensive resource for a renewable collection of the latest stories. If you already have lots of books, a small, sturdy bookshelf might be in order for your quiet corner. But even a large plastic crate can contain a number of books, and is easy to stash out of the way when necessary. Stackable crates are handy too. Some can be placed sideways to make an open shelf or stacked one on top of another. You do not want them stacked higher than a couple of feet, however.

This corner is also a natural spot for stuffed toys. A wicker laundry basket can provide an attractive, yet practical, way to keep them available for cuddling. Another item you might consider for the quiet corner is a childproof cassette player and a selection of children's tapes.

Dramatic Play

This used to be called the housekeeping corner until that became a politically incorrect term. But the fact remains, this is the space where children will dress up, "bake a cake," talk on the phone, and be a "daddy" or "mommy" or anything else their imagination can dream up. The minimal necessities for this area are a large box filled with dress-up clothes, a mirror on the wall, dolls, some kid-sized dishes, pots and pans, and a play phone. A large toy box can be a storage area. With a safety hinge (a hinge that prevents the lid from plunking down on a child's head) it can double as a bench when not in use. Of course, this area can be as elaborate as you like, with child-sized kitchen appliances, miniature foods, and tables and chairs, but these items aren't really necessary since the purpose of the corner is to encourage imaginative play. Children are great at improvising, and as we all know, necessity is the mother of invention.

You can usually procure dress-up clothes at a neighborhood garage sale or thrift shop. Search out interesting hats and shoes, flowing colorful scarves, funky purses, costume jewelry, belts, aprons, vests, gloves, frilly dresses that can be cut down so children will not trip over the hem, and anything else that looks like fun.

Dolls don't have to be fancy, but dolls' clothing can help children develop finger dexterity and teach them how to button and snap. A drawstring bag makes it easier for children to put away and find the doll clothes, and no doll should go without a baby blanket to wrap it in. (Directions for making drawstring bags are given at the end of this chapter.)

Play dishes should be unbreakable and not have too many pieces. We used a sturdy color-coordinated picnic set made by Discovery Toys. It taught children to sort according to color and pieces, and it was indestructible. Add a few pint-sized pots, pans, dish towels, and so on, and you have everything you need for a fantasy feast. These can also be stored in a large drawstring bag.

Other dramatic play toys include toy microphones, old type-writers, brooms, toy vacuum cleaners, or any prop-type toys that prompt dramatic play. Puppets are fun. Children like to watch them as well as play with them. We used to have improv puppet shows; we would make tickets and popcorn and set up chairs draped in a sheet for a theater. The only rule was you had to listen quietly to the performance (it was usually pretty slow) and then clap when it was over (somehow the clapping made everyone think the acting was great). Other impromptu forms of dramatic play are to make a train with chairs, sell tickets, and take a trip through the jungles of Africa; or create a store and play money, and "sell toys" to "customers." The possibilities are limited only by your imagination.

The Music Box

The purpose of a music box is to provide an outlet for musical expression. Fill a cardboard box or a crate with home-made items such as coffee can drums, rhythm sticks (two sticks), jingle bell bracelets (elastic with bells attached), and maracas (beans in a lidded can). You could also include colorful scarves for dancing. Other instruments might be tambourines, cymbals, triangles, recorders, kazoos, panpipes, and any other music-making devices.

Construction in Process

For obvious reasons this play zone should be located away from the quiet corner. I think *more is better* in this area. In other words, there should be lots of blocks! Building toys are the ultimate developmental toys because they grow with children. The first thing a child usually builds with blocks is a vertical tower, and he stacks them until they fall. Nothing is wrong with that; it teaches the basics of physics—gravity. Before long he tires of seeing them fall and decides to try it differently—look out Frank Lloyd Wright.

The foundation of your construction area is a set of various size wooden blocks. You might want to add a set of oversized cardboard blocks (each lightweight block is about three by six inches and can be purchased flat and assembled). Next, you need small cars and trucks, plastic animals (dinosaurs, farm critters, jungle animals), and any other accessories (miniature street signs, trees, and fences). Other playthings that fit into the construction area are sets like Legos, Construx, Playmobile, and Tinkertoys. Ideally, these toys should be stored in a visible way, perhaps on a sturdy shelf. Children can use and mix a variety of building toys, and thus the toys foster creativity. A good rule is "only take out as many toys as you plan to put away."

Use drawstring bags, plastic pails, or crates to store separate sets of construction toys and accessories. Cleanup time is as important as playtime. Children learn by sorting and putting away. A positive attitude and a place for everything can make cleanup time fun.

Arts and Crafts

At the very least, stock a cardboard box with crayons, scissors, paste, and paper. If you want a more sophisticated area, supply things like painting easels, finger-paint boards, and crafting tables. Whatever you choose, remember that creativity cannot be bought or packaged, but it can be fostered and encouraged.

A starter set for arts and crafts might include crayons (sized appropriately for ages), blunt-nosed scissors, washable ink felt-tipped pens, glue, paste or glue sticks, white paper (used computer paper works great), colored construction paper, collage materials (scraps of colored paper, macaroni, yarn, wallpaper, magazines, old greeting cards, etc.), and homemade modeling clay (see the recipe at the end of the chapter). Later you might add homemade finger paints, poster paint, paint smocks (old shirts), large paint box and brushes, a roll of butcher paper, and colored chalk and a chalkboard.

When you're thinking arts and crafts, you need to adopt a scrounge mentality. Get a big cardboard box, and stock it with toilet paper/paper towel rolls, egg cartons, Popsicle sticks, tuna fish cans, margarine tubs, yogurt/cottage cheese cartons, paper bags, newspapers, and scraps of yarn. Also watch out for natural possibilities like pinecones, leaves, and twigs.

Remember (and remind parents) that children learn by doing. The end product in artwork is not as significant as the process. In other words, do not expect Michelangelo or Picasso. Sometimes a child experiences more by smearing paste all over paper than by attaching anything to it.

I remember one boy who *never* finished his work. I would remind myself that *it's the process, not the product,* and try not to nag him. Just the same I was concerned he might be imprinted with the thought of never finishing anything. One day he was putting his unfinished project in his cubby, and I asked, "James, don't you want to finish that?" He looked at me, puzzled, and said, "I did." I nodded my head in understanding. *He was finished.* Finished was in the eyes of the beholder. I never asked again.

Science

Teaching science to young children requires nothing more than the mysteries of life and an inquisitive mind. A learning moment can occur at recess with the discovery of a gigantic spider centered on a perfectly formed web. The discussion begins with a child gasping in fear over the imposing arachnid, and your opportunity arises to share some virtues of spiders (like they help keep garden-eating bugs away). You might want a science reference book to enable you to answer questions with more knowledge, but usually, the information you have will suffice. If the children seem to have a continuing interest in, say, spiders, turn it into a unit study. Check out library books; sing "Itsy-Bitsy Spider," make spiders with black pom-poms and pipe cleaners. This works especially well in October when spiders tend to abound.

Another means of scientific learning is a science box. The contents of your box can accumulate and change over time. You and the children can collect things like sea shells, rocks, bones, pinecones, and interesting leaves. These items are even more interesting under a magnifying glass.

Other science teaching tools are aquariums, terrariums, scales for weighing, magnets and metals, an ant farm, small pets (mice, hermit crabs, etc.), cooking project materials, and a cornmeal table or a water-play table for measuring. A cornmeal table or a water-play table can be as simple as a plastic dishpan filled with cornmeal, rice, or water and some measuring cups, funnels, and various size plastic containers. Children can compare mass and weight and experience gravity while they play by manipulating the water or cornmeal. A vinyl tablecloth on the floor makes a good drop cloth for quick cleanups.

Math Toys (for four- to five-year-olds)

Math toys come in many forms, such as geo-boards, counting games, clocks, weights, measuring devices, matching games, bead stringing, abacuses, shapes, and sorting activities. These toys are geared to children over the age of three, partly for safety and also because of their developmental stage. Some of them are easy to create yourself. With a box of assorted buttons a child can count, sort by color or shape, and learn some basic math concepts. You can make a geo-board by securely nailing small finish nails into a twelve-inch-square piece of plywood; place nails in even rows, about an inch apart. Then children use colored rubberbands to create geometric shapes on the board. Another math activity is bead stringing; children can count, sort, and create patterns with beads on a string. You can make a matching card game by cutting various shapes and gluing them onto index cards (make sure you make two of each shape, and vary the colors for interest). Then children can play games matching the cards.

Not Again with the List . . .

1 Make a separate minilist for each learning center you want to incorporate (building toys, drama box, crafts).

2 Under each of these learning centers, make smaller lists: one side for "have" items and the other for "need."

3 Then if you like, compile all the need items into your shopping list to keep handy.

4 Again, shop the garage sales and secondhand stores. (Stick to the lists.)

5 Do not forget your creativity. Paint can revive many tired objects. Con-Tact paper can cover a multitude of cardboard boxes, transforming them into colorful storage containers.

Directions for making drawstring bags:

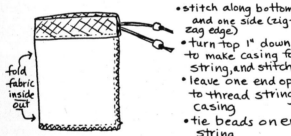

fold fabric inside out →

- stitch along bottom and one side (zig-zag edge)
- turn top 1" down to make casing for string, and stitch
- leave one end open to thread string through casing
- tie beads on ends of string

Recipe for homemade modeling clay:

1 cup flour	2 teaspoons cream of tartar
1 cup water	1 tablespoon cooking oil
½ cup salt	food color or flavoring (if desired)

Combine and mix all dry ingredients. Add food color to measured water; add water and food color slowly to dry ingredients in saucepan. Add oil and flavoring.

Cook three minutes or until mixture forms ball. Knead as soon as possible until dough is cool.

7

The Great

Outdoors

WE ALL KNOW kids need fresh air, but did you know that many pediatricians believe that children who spend at least thirty minutes outside on a daily basis, year-round, experience fewer upper respiratory virus infections (colds) than children kept indoors? Not only is fresh air healthy for the body, but it lifts the spirit as well. And an enticing play yard makes it easier to get those little ones outside. It doesn't have to be costly. I've seen children have more fun with cardboard boxes, bubble blowing, and fence painting than the most expensive play structures available.

Just the same, you'll want to consider some initial small investments. One inexpensive item, easy to locate at a neighborhood garage sale, is an exercise trampoline—you know, those circular low-to-the-ground types. It should be used on soft surfaces and monitored for safety. Swings are fun, but they require plenty of space and good supervision. If you have a tree, a climbing rope provides a way to develop the upper body. All you need is some heavy rope securely tied to a sturdy branch and knotted at one-foot intervals, reaching a couple of feet from the ground. In our playyard, most of the children only made it up the first few knots, but I remember one little guy, Brett. He was determined to climb to the top of that rope before he entered first grade. Every day Brett worked at it, gaining a little each time, until finally he made it. He was ecstatic, but more than that he had learned that if he worked hard enough, he could accomplish what had seemed an almost impossible task.

Climbing structures are good for large-muscle development. They can come in many forms, from multileveled forts, complete with ladders, slides, and climbing ropes, to a set of wooden steps. Plans or kits are usually easy to construct, especially if you have a handyperson around to help. Of course, once again safety must be a primary consideration. Any platform higher than two feet should have a safety rail. Structures must be sturdy, free from slivers or sharp edges.

Basically, common sense should be your guide with all kid equipment, but keep in mind that children do the craziest stunts. I remember we had a tire swing for a while, and some of the older children liked to twist it to give the rider a spin. We enforced a five-twist limit (this helped with counting as well as with safety). Then one day Sarah got carried away and twisted it a lot more than five times. Her friend, Charisa, was on the tire, whirling like crazy, but apparently having a great time. I walked over to remind them about five-twist rule when suddenly Charisa screamed hysterically. I realized her long hair had entwined into the twisted rope and was being tightly pulled. I stopped the spinning tire (no small stunt) and proceeded to unwind Charisa. I extracted her snarled hair while she continued to scream at the top of her lungs. Needless to say it was not much fun, and Charisa emerged with a little less hair. From that time twisting the rope was strictly forbidden.

Sandboxes can provide truckloads of fun, but they should be covered when not in use (at least if any cats live within, say, a hundred-mile radius). We used a lightweight piece of garden lattice to cover our sandbox. The biggest problem with sand, besides throwing, is getting it out of clothing. I always tried to close the sandbox about ten minutes before we went inside.

That gave the kids a chance to bounce some of the sand off first. (For sand in the eye, a few drops of milk in the affected eye will coagulate the sand so it can be removed easily.)

Other inexpensive outside toys and activities:

- Hula hoops (for rolling and jumping)
- Balls (soccer, plastic baseball, soft football)
- Small (automobile) tires to stack or roll
- Wheel toys (trikes, wagons, wheelbarrows, etc.)
- Bubble blowing (Make bubble solution from diluted liquid dish soap and bubble sticks from twisted wire.)
- Fence painting (Use cheap two-inch paintbrushes from the hardware store dipped into water containers made from tin cans.) The kids can then paint dry light-toned wood of a fence, house, shed, or whatever to create dark wet streaks. It's cheap fun, plus they develop eye-hand coordination and artistic expression.

In the summer, offer water play outside. You need only a wading pool, lots of containers and utensils for pouring and measuring, and several inches of water. You can add food coloring or bubbles. Even with only a few inches of water, play with these containers requires close supervision, and the "pools" should be emptied after each use. The summer is a good time to take some traditionally indoor activities outside, which can also help beat the summer blahs. A coloring table placed in the sun can produce interesting pictures because solar heat softens crayon wax, resulting in extra vibrant colors. We also had fun creating an outdoor puppet theater by painting and decorating a big appliance box. Big boxes can also become spaceships, houses, stores, and submarines, and several smaller boxes linked together can form a train. Make sure any sharp staples are removed. Picnics and tea parties with dolls and dress-up clothes are lots more fun outside.

Games like hoop toss, beanbag throw, and basketball can

be made or purchased, and they work well outside. A plastic garbage can with a tight-fitting lid is a good place to store smaller outdoor toys. Just tip it on its side for children to retrieve objects.

If you have a spare corner you don't mind spading, a small garden can be an excellent way to teach science and nutrition (it's amazing what children will eat if they grow it themselves). Or wooden boxes filled with soil can contain individual raised garden beds. Our garden consisted mostly of strawberries, tomatoes, and flowers, but the children enjoyed it immensely. There is a special delight in discovering something new blooming in the garden or eating a strawberry dipped in dew, right off the vine.

Sometimes, if it's very cold, children will tend to stand around in the playyard. That's a good time for a quick walk. Naturally, you need a safe walking environment, but this is a wonderful way to get the children out for a breath of fresh air. It is also an excellent opportunity to observe seasonal changes, talk about safety, and teach the children to walk as a group. If the children are inexperienced at staying together, you might try being a "caterpillar." Take a length of rope and tell the children to hold on to it to create a caterpillar (make sure there is enough room between children so they don't trip over one another's feet). It also works well to have children walk with partners.

Children often learn to either appreciate or disdain activities from the adults they are with. If the adult does not like going outdoors, the child will likely have little interest as well. We need to impart healthy habits and attitudes to young children. We do not want to raise a fresh crop of couch potatoes, or tater tots as I tend to call them. Besides, as a caregiver, you need fresh air and exercise just as much as your little charges. And at the end of the day, I have never heard anyone complain about the time wasted out in the fresh air or the moment spent to smell the roses.

8

Business with a *B*:
What to Do Before
You Open Your Doors

I AM NOT by nature a businesswoman. Consistent record keeping, organization, and bookkeeping are not my forte. Just ask my husband. Fortunately, there is hope for people like me—and you, too, if you can relate. It is also comforting to know, especially for those of us who tremble in fear at terms like *accounting, bookkeeping,* or, heaven forbid, a *tax audit,* these are not the essentials for providing excellent childcare. The key to becoming a good businesswoman is to keep it simple. And before you agree to take in anyone else's child, you should carefully consider the following prerequisites for success.

Be Prepared

We have already discussed how to prepare your home and yard for providing childcare. But there are ways you can prepare yourself. First of all, start thinking of yourself as a *professional.* Basically, that is someone who gets paid for skills and services— and isn't that what you plan to do? If you still feel insecure about your specific expertise in early childhood education, go ahead and bone up as you prepare to open your childcare business.

Libraries and bookstores have plenty of resources available on the subject of child development.

Special, but Simple, Training

This is also an excellent time to check out first aid/CPR classes. Many hospitals, community centers, and colleges offer these classes in one-day sessions; some are even designed to focus on young children. Even if you decide not to provide childcare, having first aid training can be useful in any of life's arenas.

You could also find out if your state offers food handler's certification. It is usually regulated by the Department of Health and Human Services, and is often mandatory for restaurant workers. If your state requires this certification, you will first study a fact-filled pamphlet about food storage, preparation, hygiene, and so on. Then you'll take a quick exam to receive a food handler's card.

Post your first aid certificate and food handler's card where prospective parents can see them when they look into your services before enrollment. (A small portable bulletin board works well for this, and it can be stashed on weekends if you want to reduce clutter.) By displaying these cards, you exhibit your professionalism to parents, and you give reassurance that their children will be in good hands. Your bulletin board should also display things like the weekly menu, the schedule, and a copy of your policy.

"My Policy?"

Establish your policy before you announce your intent to provide care. This is a written document to give each parent as well as post in a visible place (like your bulletin board). It clarifies what parents can expect from you, and what you, in turn, can expect from them. A policy includes: daily hours, holidays off, payment procedures, discipline methods, and the plan to deal with illness. You may want individual policies for some of these things. A written policy protects you by removing any unknown factors. For instance, if a parent questions why you are not open the day before Christmas, you can point to your policy and say, "As you can see, it says right here we are closed December 24." That settles it. Or as Judge Wapner says, "Put it in writing."

"How, and How Much, Do I Charge?"

Another major section of your policy, and something you need to consider at this time, is your tuition fees and billing procedure. The best way to establish your tuition is to call around and find out the going rate in your area. The cost varies by region. Chances are, you'll discover a wide range of fees depending on the type of care. Infant care is always more; state-run centers like Head Start will naturally be less since they are subsidized with tax dollars. Corporate care (that is, childcare businesses that house multitudes of children) tends to be the most expensive, however, most child development specialists agree this style of childcare does not necessarily represent the best quality care.

You need to evaluate how the care you intend to provide compares to what is already out there. But don't sell yourself short, and don't expect to increase your tuition within the first year. After a year you may want to reevaluate and raise your fees only if other providers in your area are increasing theirs.

There are several ways to charge: hourly, daily, weekly, or monthly. In all instances you're wise to require either prepayment or daily payment. I made it my policy to *never* allow anyone to get behind on payments. I'd heard too many stories about childcare providers working out of their homes and not getting paid.

I found it simplest to offer three basic choices: (1) monthly, (2) weekly, and (3) hourly only with drop-ins (and the drop-ins were always personal friends who only occasionally used my services). The monthly rate was by far the best buy. For those who paid monthly, I required one month's tuition in advance: this protects you from nonpayment or unexpected dropouts. For the parents, it secures their child's place in your facility and saves them money. For those who paid the more expensive weekly rate, I required them to pay one or two weeks in advance. I also reminded them their child's place wasn't guaranteed beyond two weeks (in case a full-time opening was needed by another family willing to commit to the monthly agreement). This policy encourages parents to commit to your care, or it allows someone else to. And that gives you more security as a businesswoman.

For belated payments, my policy required a late fee, but I never needed to implement it. Occasionally, a parent had a justifiable excuse, and I would choose to overlook the late fee. Naturally, circumstances arise when you can afford to be charitable. For instance, one single mom was trying to go to school and keep her three children fed and clothed, and one child required part-time care. Although her childcare was partially subsidized, the rest came out of her pocket. After several late notices, I told her not to worry about her extra payment; it was not a lot anyway. Business was going well and I wanted to help her out. Being able to make those kinds of choices, I believe, is one of the best perks of running your own business.

Just the same, there are some *deadbeats* (parents who move their children from place to place, piling up unpaid bills). You do them, and yourself, no favors by allowing them to take advantage of you. So if a stringent prepaid tuition plan seems hard-nosed now, remember it pays off in the long run with peace of mind and respect from the parents for your businesslike professionalism.

Some care providers ask parents to sign and return a copy of the policy, guaranteeing they have read and understood its contents. This procedure protects your rights, and in this lawsuit-hungry day and age, it never hurts to be extra prepared. In all my years of providing childcare, I never needed to seek out legal counsel, but that's a decision providers should make for themselves.

Be Organized

I have always disliked the sound of the word *organized*. But the truth is, it's not that hard to be organized. Being organized means having a workable system for keeping your records straight and accessible. Organization simplifies your job and your life. And if you spend a little extra time with a preliminary setup, it will pay off in big dividends, like peace of mind, later.

When I decided to provide childcare at home, the first thing I bought was a used two-drawer file cabinet. I spray painted it and stenciled across the front of the drawers (my husband thought that was silly), but somehow making it attractive made it easier for me to put it to use.

I bought a big box of file folders and labeled them with everything I could think of from *A* to *Z* regarding childcare. Many of them were for copies of forms I planned to keep on hand: medical release forms, field trip slips, immunization forms, medication permission slips, and enrollment forms. Some files were for tax-deductible receipts: organized by food, supplies, repair, and such. Other files held menu ideas, first aid, food handling, and poison control information, and miscellaneous items. Then I set aside a clientele section where each child would have an individual file to hold completed enrollment forms, immunization records, permission slips, and any other pertinent information I might need. I created files for my personal interests: gardening ideas, craft projects, and the like. I also made files for each of my children; it was a handy place to stash their important papers. These all went into the top drawer.

I used the lower drawer for curriculum ideas and projects. I organized them according to the months, and I included seasonal ideas and different themes I intended to use throughout the year. I am not saying this file cabinet system will change your life, but it could simplify things, and if you don't already use a filing system, it's time to start.

Be a Record Keeper

The simpler your daily record-keeping system, the easier it is to maintain over the long run. My favorite system is an ordinary three-ring binder notebook with several dividers.

Emergency Phone Numbers

I always kept each child's emergency phone numbers taped to the inside cover of this notebook. I also kept a list by the phone, in my car, and in the file. It may have been overkill on my part, but I felt better having them readily available, especially when someone else might temporarily relieve me.

Sign-in Section

The first section of your notebook holds daily sign-in sheets. Here you keep track of dates and times children are in your care, which is very important for tax purposes and USDA food reimbursements (see Chapter 11). Some providers like parents to sign in their own children. In that case you might keep a separate spiral notebook by the entry. The only problem with this system is that parents often forget. To make it work, you must train the parents to sign in and out, and you must double-check that they do.

Accident Reports

Another section should contain accident reports. Use it whenever a child is injured while in your care. The accident report must include the date and time, the child's name, how she got hurt, and any first aid treatment administered. If you notice an injury that did *not* occur while the child was in your care, you could note it here, including the date, the description of the injury, and how the child says the injury occurred. This information is vital should you begin to see a pattern or suspect abuse; these records can become important documentation if you need to make a report to authorities. Not only that, these records could protect you from false accusations.

Medicine Log

You will need a medicine log for administering any medication (even children's Tylenol), and you will only give medicine when you have written parental permission to do so. In this section you will also record the child's name, the date and time, the type and amount of medicine given, and the reason for the medicine.

Be a Planner

I am sure you have heard this one before: "Those who fail to plan, plan to fail." Trite as it may sound, it can be painfully true with a childcare business. Caring for children is challenging at best, and lack of planning can drive you bananas. So get mentally ready to become a planner. Here is a quick overview of the three main areas that will require some planning.

1. Daily Schedule

Your daily schedule is actually a timetable for when to do things like serve snacks, have recess, and start naptime. It can be compared to an understructure you build your day upon. Without some sort of schedule your day will eventually sag and quite possibly collapse. (There will be more tips for creating a successful schedule in Chapter 10.)

2. Menu Planning

Menu planning is essential because eating is such a big part of a child's day, and the menu plan provides you with your shopping guide. Most moms know that feeling of frustration when five o'clock rolls around and you don't know what you're fixing for dinner. Multiply that several times if you don't know what's for lunch and a bunch of kids are saying, "I'm hungry." (Chapter 11 will give you some specific ideas for menu planning.)

3. Curriculum

By curriculum, I refer to what I call theme-style learning. You pick daily, weekly, or monthly themes and build your activities around them. For instance, if your week's theme is color, you might plan a science project like mixing water and food coloring to create new colors, or you might declare a "green day" when everyone wears green. These themes give you a focus as you select library books, art projects, field trips, science activities, and such. (Appendix C is filled with curriculum ideas.)

The whole point with planning is that although it need not be complicated, it is the main ingredient for success. We need to recognize our plans as foundational, and we might even rephrase that planning adage to a more positive note by saying, "Those who build a plan, plan to build."

Summary

1   Look into attaining first aid, and food handler's certification.
Read up on child development.

2   Plan your childcare policies:
a. Payment structure
b. Hours open; holidays off
c. Illness procedures
d. Discipline

3   Create an easy-to-use filing system and make forms:
a. Enrollment forms
b. Immunization forms
c. Medical releases
d. Child's records
e. Field trip permits
f. Menus
g. USDA records
h. Food handler's certificate
i. First aid
j. Curriculum ideas
k. Tax records
l. And much more!

4   Plan a handy record notebook for daily use:
a. Sign-in sheets
b. Accident reports
c. Medicine log
d. Daily schedule
e. Menu
f. Curriculum plan
g. Emergency phone numbers

9

Image Building:
If You Build It,
Will They Come?

YOU HAVE UNCLUTTERED your home, your policy is written, you are fired up and ready to go, but what if you don't get any little customers? If recent statistics are accurate, about half the mothers in the U.S. work outside the home. In other words, you have a ready-made market out there waiting for you. But how do you find them? How do you get the word out?

The best advertising is always word of mouth. When a friend recommends a new product, aren't you more likely to try it? We all appreciate the comfort of familiarity. You feel safer hiring Joe Blow, the plumber, when you know he's your neighbor's brother. This is even more true with childcare. It's not hard to understand how most parents want to know and trust those who provide care for their children. I found by mentioning my new enterprise to a few friends, I instantly accumulated enough customers to open my doors.

You'll find clientele sources with your neighbors, friends, and relatives. Just remember to let them know—it's up to you to spread the news. Maybe Betty Lou, down the street, has a niece looking for a reliable person to care for little Suzy.

After you've let the word out, give it some time. Even people who want to switch over to your care must usually give at least two weeks' notice to their current childcare provider. However, if things are moving too slowly, you might post a colorful flyer on your church bulletin board. Or if you live in a neighborhood where people keep to themselves, you might consider placing an attractive sign outside your home. You could make it like an announcement to inform your neighbors that you'll soon provide childcare, and that you welcome them to stop by. This has a twofold purpose: First, when you operate a home-based business, you need the support of your neighborhood. You need to be a good neighbor and answer any concerns they may have about noise, parking, and such. Second, reassure them that your business will not have a negative impact on the neighborhood; in fact, it will become an asset.

If you're still waiting for customers after many weeks, you might post a flyer at your neighborhood market or take out an ad in the classifieds. But remember, at this point you're recruiting from people you don't know. The children and parents you provide care for will become like your own family. You want to feel secure about establishing both a personal and a professional relationship with them. This is the time for them to thoroughly read your written policies and make sure they agree with your basic childcare philosophy. Also you'll want them to fill out a background information form. After all, you'll be partners with them. You'll essentially become a part-time parent to their child. When dealing with a complete stranger, you may wish to request a childcare or personal reference. A conscientious parent will respect your professionalism and will probably want your references as well. Prepare a small list of friends, employers, and/or pastors who would be willing to take a phone call on your behalf.

A Book by Its Cover

We do it all the time. If the restaurant looks dirty, we don't want to eat there. How much more stringent would we be in selecting childcare for *our* children? You should expect most parents to take a long hard look at your place—and you. Their judgments may not necessarily be fair, or the parents may misinterpret what they see. But it's still up to you to put your best foot forward.

We've already established that it's time to eliminate clutter purely for safety purposes, but you'll also want to take into account the aesthetic appearance of your home. Does it present a bright and cheery face? Do your windows shine? Are the window coverings fresh and neat? Sometimes a pot of blooming flowers on the front step works wonders, and it helps if you keep your walk swept clean. How about a colorful (non-slip) rug in the entry, a pleasant picture on the wall (at child height), or some bright perky pillows on the couch? How does your house smell? Is it stuffy and stale? Crack a window; spray some room freshener; do whatever it takes to give the feel, as well as the look, of cleanliness and order. After all, these small things send a big message: *someone here cares.* One tip I always give parents who are looking into various childcare facilities is to check out the bathrooms and kitchen for cleanliness. So be ready. Someone may want to see *your* bathroom.

Maybe your home is due for some fresh paint or new carpeting anyway. It will be easier to make these changes *before* you start providing care. Choose a hardy scrubbable paint and a tough stain-resistant carpet (the best carpet for hiding almost *anything* is a middle-toned neutral, like gray, taupe, or beige, in a short nap). Another quick and easy perk up for the exterior of your home is to paint your front door in a pleasing color and hang a welcoming decoration close by. Any improvements you make directly related to your childcare business can usually be deducted from your taxes as a business expense (just remember to save those receipts). So why not take advantage of sprucing up for business' sake, and give a gift to your family at the same time?

Looking the Part

One benefit of working at home is the money you save on a working wardrobe. But that does not mean you should wear old grungy sweats and bedroom slippers every day. As comfy as that getup may sound, it doesn't present a very professional image. You want parents to take your role seriously. You're not just the gum-chewing baby-sitter anymore.

Personally, I find when I hang out in sloppy sweats all day, I start to feel the way I look, and consequently, it affects my perspective. Taking an extra few minutes to pull myself together usually improves the quality of my entire day. Not only do parents notice the difference, but the children do too.

Children appreciate fun and colorful fashion statements, even if it is something as simple as pumpkin earrings on Halloween. How you take care of yourself sends a message. The message can be, "This job stinks," or "I think my occupation is important enough to look good."

Does this mean you need a whole new wardrobe? Probably not, but a few new working clothes might be a nice perk of earning extra money. Naturally, you'll want clothes that are as comfortable and washable as they are attractive. Sticky fingers and unexpected messes are inevitable and always less stressful when you know you can throw that outfit into the wash without batting an eyelash. These days, with the advent of cotton knits and the social acceptability of jeans, dressing for success in the field of childcare isn't too difficult.

To market any business, you should appreciate the importance of *image*. Then you can focus on the things that really matter, such as what do I do with all these children now that they are here?

Summary

1 How to get your childcare clientele:
   a. Friends and word of mouth
   b. Church/flyer on bulletin board
   c. Neighborhood/small nice sign
   d. Neighborhood market/flyer
   e. Local newspaper ad (last resource)

2 Give your home a face-lift:
   a. Improved curb appeal and front door/entry
   b. Clean, colorful, and cheerful inside

3 Put your best foot forward:
   a. Have your references ready
   b. Have your policy available
   c. Look like a childcare professional

10

The
Schedule

CHILDREN ARE SO spontaneous and even unpredictable. It seems they always do the unexpected, and yet at the same time, they actually thrive on routine. Knowing *what happens next* gives them a very real sense of security, and this seemingly small assurance is vital to children being cared for outside their homes. It fosters within them a feeling of control in what might otherwise seem a foreign or perhaps hostile world. Children gain certain power by knowing, for instance, that recess follows snacktime. Having that information makes them feel important, which, in turn, boosts self-esteem.

A secondary, but equally essential, goal of a good childcare provider is to encourage emotionally healthy and capable children. To this end, a daily schedule is not merely a convenience; it's a requirement. But before we plunge completely into schedules . . .

Let's Be on the Lookout for Serendipities

You see, no daily schedule should ever be carved in stone. Another advantage of being your own boss is your daily opportunity for flexibility. There will be times you'll want to capitalize on the moment—take a break from routine and experience a serendipity (*serendipity* is defined as "an unplanned moment of delightful discovery").

For instance, after recess, you're going in for lunch when Jenny discovers a big fuzzy caterpillar. Why not let all the children examine the critter? Perhaps bring out the magnifying glass. Maybe you'll put it in a big pickle jar so the children can observe it create a cocoon in the following weeks. Maybe you have a storybook about caterpillars (e.g., *The Hungry Caterpillar*). Or you might plan a special craft project for after naptime (e.g., egg carton caterpillars). In other words, seize the moment, and work these teachable times into your daily routine.

Now Back to Schedules

A good schedule will balance a child's day with an appropriate mix of both quiet and lively activities. If your day starts early in the morning, you may want to begin slowly with quiet activities as the children arrive. You might want to offer "talking" books (books with cassette tapes) or perhaps a subdued children's video. If you're lucky, a quiet educational show like *Mister Rogers' Neighborhood* may be on the air. Remember children need time to make the transition from home to childcare. Maybe it's been a hectic morning for them, or maybe they've not fully awake and just need to curl up with a blanket on the couch.

Free Playtime

As the morning progresses you can offer more choices by opening up the various *learning centers* (as discussed in Chapter 6). You can also expect the noise level to increase. It requires supervision to keep children interested in different activities, but it's also possible to fold a basket of laundry at the same time. This is when children practice self-motivation, and have their chance to share and take turns. Although it's an independent playtime, they require some direction and intermediate intervention. By "intermediate intervention," I refer to settling differences like: "Jordan took my dinosaur and I'm gonna punch him if he doesn't give it back." You need to intervene, but your goal is to teach sharing and communication, and to show them how to get along without constantly crying out for teacher to solve every dispute. Free playtime is when children develop coping and social skills.

I've seen well-meaning providers who have tried to format every minute of the day, never allowing for free choice or unstructured playtime. By doing this, children are robbed of their autonomy (independence, self-reliance), and they learn to be adult-dependent for all of their entertainment.

Living in a work-oriented society, some people transfer their adult values into the child's world. Some parents expect their young children to achieve unrealistic academic success. Some parents would be proud to have their three-year-olds speaking fluent French and doing multiplication tables. Yet we need to remember, *a child's work is to play*. The fact is, while at free play, children learn by hands-on experience some very important concepts. For instance, by forcing a preschooler to sit and write out numerals instead of playing with blocks, an adult can cause the child to miss the opportunity to learn about gravity, engineering, cause and effect, and consequential reasoning, not to mention developing small motor skills. This is called *developmental learning*. Since each child develops at a unique pace, free play allows a child to choose the activity that is appropriate to her stage of development. Never feel apologetic about the slots on your schedule for free playtime. Or if it really bothers you, call them *developmental activities*.

Cleanup Time

Always allot plenty of time for picking up. Cleanup time is as important as free playtime. Picking up teaches personal responsibility (you played with it; you put it away). It also provides a training ground for developmental skills like sorting, classification, and organized thinking. You could spend big bucks to buy educational games to teach those skills, or you could simply encourage children to clean up.

You can handle cleanup time like a special event (not drudgery) by making it into a game. That way you won't just avoid the whining "I don't-wanna's"; you'll also help your little charges get on track with a good attitude toward accountability. How do you make it into a game? Try counting blocks as they land in the crate or sorting items by color or shape. Play music while they pick up, stopping it occasionally. When the music stops, the children freeze, and you can compliment them on their work. You can give stickers as awards for good cleaning. Be creative.

Snack Time

When you schedule your midmorning snack (or any eating time), always set aside a few minutes for *supervised* hand washing first (supervised, that is, until you are satisfied the children know how to properly cleanse their hands). Morning snack time is also a sharing and socializing event.

Circle Time

Include a daily story time, or what many centers call circle time, in your routine. Children love hearing stories, and this is a direct predecessor to teaching reading. It is a fact: young children who are read to regularly learn to read sooner than those who are not. The best storybooks only have a few sentences on each page and large easy-to-see pictures. A good storyteller should speak clearly, use a little dramatic flair, and exaggerate facial expressions. Children love sound effects, whether it's lowering your voice to a whisper in a mysterious section, or booming like Paul Bunyan and imitating a tree crashing to the ground. In short, pretend you are performing on stage (to an audience who adores you). With storytime, you can teach children to love books and, in turn, to love reading. It would be costly to keep an inexhaustible picture book selection on hand, so invite children to bring books from home, and plan regular library trips. Many libraries will allow ten to twenty books per visit if you provide childcare.

If you have adequate transportation for the children in your care, you might consider making an annual library outing with them. Many libraries offer a weekly story hour, which is often accompanied by puppetry, props, or small craft projects. The children are enriched, they get a chance to exchange books, and you get a short break.

Circle time is also an appropriate time for action rhymes, songs, and fingerplays (rhymes you act out with your hands). The developmental purpose behind these rhymes and songs is multifaceted, starting with language and memory development, eye-hand control, finger dexterity, attention training, rhythm, and musical exposure. But perhaps the best reason is simply because they're fun. Children enjoy this time, and the chance to join together in creative expression. I'll include some tried-and-true favorites in Appendix B, and the more seasonal ones are mentioned in Appendix C.

Show-and-tell is a circle time event that allows a child to communicate with the group without interruption. Some quieter children don't often get the floor to themselves. It also gives you an inside glimpse into their home lives, habits, pets, siblings, and such. They often share an object of interest from home or an experience—sometimes real, sometimes not. Young children tend to perceive a blurry line between reality and fantasy. Show and tell is your chance to encourage language development, not to make a judgment on content.

Recess

A morning recess works nicely right before lunch. By that time, children are ready for some hardy exercise, and the dew is usually off the grass. Again, this is mostly an unstructured outdoor playtime. If you have an adequate play yard, children should be content to play. Sometimes they may need encouragement from you, but your main goal should be to help them play independently. Obviously, it should be an active time, a time for large-muscle development. Some skills you might encourage include hopping, skipping, jumping, running, galloping, climbing, and such. Remember, though, each child develops at a unique pace. Not all children will be able to do all those things. One way to help children master these skills is in noncompetitive relay races. Line up the children, and let them take turns hopping like bunnies or galloping like horses to the fence and back.

After Recess

Another reason for having recess before lunch is that children usually need to wash up after a vigorous outdoor play session anyway, and this prepares them for lunch (killing two birds with one stone). It almost goes without saying how fresh air and lively play also enhance appetites.

Pre-lunch

You may require a few minutes to pull lunch together. One surefire method is to pop in a children's video to occupy them for a few minutes. Another idea is to have "library time" by encouraging them to look at books independently. This quiet activity helps them to change gears and settle down after a rip-roaring recess.

Lunch

Lunch is usually a highlight for most children. It's a fun and social time to gather and enjoy good food. Some centers encourage children to serve themselves family style. This develops coordination and helps children estimate how much they can eat, but I must admit, I never cared for it. For sanitation's sake and ease, I chose to serve the children myself. I knew just how much they had or had not had, and I didn't worry about food contamination. Young children naturally tend to lick serving spoons and use fingers. (See Chapter 11 for food ideas.)

Naptime

Naptime is a natural sequence to lunch, especially after a busy morning and a meal. A short word of warning: never use naptime as a consequence for misbehavior. If you do, you might create a naptime nightmare. You want children to look forward to resting, whenever possible, or at least not to hate it. Refer to naptime in a positive manner, and you will have much less balking when it's time to head for bed. One way to ease into naptime is to allow quiet book reading on cots or mats for the first ten minutes. This works well when children are taking turns to use the bathroom, and helps them wind down. A semidarkened room and soft, soothing music can set a peaceful mood for a successful rest time.

I always made a point of telling children, "You don't have to go to sleep. Just rest quietly for a while." Nine times out of ten, they were snoozing within minutes. You may wish to post a note on your entry door for parents to enter quietly while children are at rest. Another rest-time precaution is to use an answering machine with the sound turned off and placed on automatic answer. That way, you can receive calls without noisy interruptions. Naptime is usually one to two and a half hours, depending on the children. As they awaken, you can offer quiet activities (puzzles, books, learning toys) until everyone is awake.

The Rest of the Day

The remainder of the afternoon can be filled with an afternoon snack, recess, free play, and so on. Bear in mind the need to balance lively and quiet activities as you schedule the day. You might try graphing your daily schedule's lively versus quiet times. They should rise and fall like gently rolling waves. You do not want to experience a dead calm followed by the massive typhoon that wipes everyone out, including you.

If you keep children after five o'clock, you may want to offer a late afternoon snack or a light dinner (if prearranged with the parent). Your schedule, for a great part, will naturally evolve around regular eating intervals. Children have small-capacity stomachs, and they function better with slighter portions every two to three hours.

After you've decided on the schedule that works best for you, post it for parents to easily view, and give them their own copies. Parents feel more comfortable to visit if they know what you are doing at certain periods of the day. You want to encourage parents to visit at any time. They gain a sense of security by knowing you have nothing to hide. Naturally, there are times when it's less convenient for visits. Most parents will be considerate of this factor, but you should *never* tell them *not* to visit during any specific portion of the day. If a care provider said such a thing to me, that would be exactly when I'd go to visit. Wouldn't you? Keep an open-door policy, and you'll build a healthy foundation of trust.

Schedule (Sample)

7:30 A.M.	Children arrive, books, videos, quiet activities
8:00 A.M.	Breakfast time (optional)
8:30 A.M.	Free play, learning centers
10:00 A.M.	Wash hands
10:10 A.M.	Morning snack time
10:30 A.M.	Circle time
10:50 A.M.	Recess
11:50 A.M.	Come inside, wash hands
12:00 P.M.	Lunchtime
12:30 P.M.	Rest time
2:30 P.M.	Afternoon snack time
3:00 P.M.	Recess
4:00 P.M.	Free play
5:00 P.M.	Evening snack (or dinner)
6:00 P.M.	Good-bye!

11

They Eat
and Eat

"WHEN'S IT GONNA be snack time?" they'll ask, knowing full well it's at ten o'clock like any other day. Eating is very important to children—not merely for the nutritional value, but also because it's a social time. They like sitting around the table, swapping tall tales with their buddies. Some may be picky, but most kids enjoy eating.

The first year I provided care, planning meals almost drove me crazy. I thought I should fix a wide variety of hearty dishes. Unfortunately, much of that food wound up in the garbage—even the dog wouldn't eat my tuna casserole. Finally, it dawned on me: children do not really appreciate the unusual, the diverse, or anything new when it comes to kid cuisine. The fact is, most children prefer familiar foods. Some kids would happily consume peanut butter sandwiches morning, noon, and night (not that I recommend it, although peanut butter certainly has its place on the childcare menu).

The answer to my dining dilemma came in the form of a two-week rotating menu. This menu included all of what I had discovered to be kid-favored foods, following a period of trial and error. Another benefit of this two-week plan is simplified shopping. You can use the same list again and again, perhaps with some variation when it comes to seasonal foods or a good buy. If you belong to a warehouse-type store, you can purchase supplies in bulk and thus eliminate extra trips (you can also deduct your membership fee as a business expense as well as your mileage back and forth—do not forget to save all those receipts). I must admit my two-week menu plan seemed a bit boring to me, as an adult, but the point is, the children liked it, and they ate well. They would request seconds and thirds, and rarely did the dog see any leftovers.

The first thing I found is that children like to identify and recognize exactly what they are eating. They might pick at a Waldorf salad, but they would happily devour any of those salad ingredients served separately. The same thing is true with casseroles. Take my tuna casserole. I could bake some tuna, noodles, celery, and maybe cheese on top, and they'd say, "YUCK!" But when I served tuna sandwiches with celery sticks and a wedge of cheese, I could watch it disappear. Now some might say, "You're just spoiling those kids. They should eat grown-up foods like the rest of us." To this I ask, "Why?" What possible good can result in a child taking one sample bite, turning up his nose, and throwing the rest of his lunch in the trash can? For me, a priority in providing quality care includes making absolutely certain the children consume adequate quantities of healthful food. And that means offering foods with child appeal.

We need to respect that most children appreciate simplicity, and we can then appreciate how that, in turn, makes food preparation simpler for us. Finger foods are always popular. Carrot sticks vanish before your eyes, while cooked carrots must often be scraped off the plate into the garbage. That brings us to other advantages of finger foods: easier cleanup, fewer slimy plates, and often no forks or spoons to wash. Of course, I did not serve everything raw. There were times, especially in winter, when cooked foods were welcome to warm small tummies. But for the most part I let the children be my guide, keeping the basics of good nutrition as the rule.

Nutrition Basics

You have surely heard of the four basic food groups, but do you know how much to serve from each group? One way is to imagine the food groups stacked up like a pyramid (starting with the bread group as the largest portion on the bottom and the meat group as the smallest one on the top).

The serving sizes suggested in the following groups are child-sized portions, and therefore may seem like more food than necessary. But consider when a child drinks orange juice, it might be only four ounces.

Bread, Cereal, and Grains Group

The bread, cereal, and grains food group provides the base of our food pyramid. It's like the foundation, and growing bodies need more servings from this group than any other, about four to six per day. This is also a high-carbohydrate group. That's the fuel that keeps our engines running, and as we know, children's engines run hard and fast. Fortunately, this group is probably the most popular with children. You can always get even the most finicky child to eat a slice of bread with jam or a bowl of cereal. Although whole grains are healthier, many children do not naturally seem to like them. I introduced children to whole wheat bread by serving it toasted (it was less obvious that it wasn't white). One hint to introduce a new food is to pair it with something they already know and love. Peanut butter works wonders here. It's amazing how you can slap peanut butter on all sorts of things to entice children to try new foods.

Fruit and Vegetable Group

The next group contains fruits and vegetables; a suggested minimum is three to four servings a day. In this group, more is better. These foods are loaded with natural vitamins and fiber. Although we all know it is tough to get kids to eat their vegetables, I have seen them try things like zucchini, broccoli, and even cauliflower, when it's cut into finger foods, served raw, and dipped into a ranch-style yogurt dressing. When it comes to cooked vegetables, corn, peas, and potatoes were about the only ones I had much success with.

Now fruit is a different story. It's always a cinch to get children to eat fruit, whether it is fresh, canned, or in juice form. Fresh produce is almost always your best bet nutritionally (and often financially). Not only that, fresh fruits and vegetables contain more fiber than processed foods, and fiber is something most children do not get enough of anyway.

Dairy Group

The next group is milk products, and the minimal requirement is about three servings a day. You can also use this group as a substitute for the protein group, especially when combined with a grain product. For instance, macaroni with real cheese and milk constitutes as much protein as many meat products. We tend to think of meat and poultry as the best form of protein, but we need to recognize that combining grains and legumes with milk products can equal or surpass many of those foods. Many nutritionists think these foods are easier on the digestive system. Of course, the best way to furnish dairy products is through milk, and I recommend serving milk with each meal.

Protein Group

The final group at the peak of the pyramid (the smallest part, meaning we require the least) is the meat, fish, and poultry group (or protein). We can get by with two to three servings from this group daily. Unfortunately, Americans have in the past inverted this pyramid and consumed more from this group than is necessary or even healthy. The good news here, for a childcare provider, is that you do not need to focus greatly on this group, and that means less preparation time and less cost.

Part of our responsibility in caring for children is to teach good nutrition by providing wholesome and balanced meals and snacks. Children do not necessarily understand the nutritional difference between a can of pop and a can of fruit juice. They just know both taste good and quench their thirst. It is up to us to educate them and explain why fruit juice actually helps their bodies grow, but pop is loaded with sugar and has absolutely no nutritional value.

I remember when my son was small and asked if he could pick out some gum at the supermarket checkout.

"Only if it is sugarless," I replied, absently unloading my cart. He soon proudly plopped down a bright-colored package.

"This has sugar in it," I explained, knowing he could not read the label. He smiled and nodded. "But I said sugarless," I repeated, emphasing the "less."

"Yep, Mom," he said proudly. "It has *sugarless* in it." Suddenly, I realized he thought *sugarless* meant it *had* sugar. The term *sugarless* meant nothing to him. So many times we assume children understand, without remembering their limited scope of experience or their childlike perspectives. So it may take some explaining why Goo-Goo Puff cereal is not really *good* for you, even though junior thinks it tastes *good*. To him, good is good. What could be simpler?

Breakfast in a Cup

We always hear that "breakfast is the most important meal of the day." Consequently, when I first started offering breakfast as a childcare option for my early birds, I tried to make it hearty. But after the dog enjoyed yet another generous serving of bacon and eggs, I decided to reevaluate. Most young children do not have a huge appetite first thing in the morning. And in childcare, they'll have another snack in a couple of hours anyway. Therefore, I started thinking of breakfast more like a big snack. That was when I discovered four ounce Dixie cups. For some reason fruit-flavored yogurt tasted better when eaten from a little Dixie cup. Don't ask me why. Or sometimes I would put dry cereal in a Dixie cup, fill another one with milk, and offer a fruit wedge on the side. The children devoured these snack-sized breakfasts.

The nutritional formula for a simple breakfast is one grain product serving, one dairy product serving, and one fruit or vegetable serving.

Two Weeks of Simple Breakfast Ideas

1. Bagel, yogurt, orange juice
2. Cinnamon toast, milk, banana
3. Cheerios, milk, apple wedges
4. Muffin, cocoa, orange slices
5. Granola, milk, peaches
6. Toast, yogurt, apple juice
7. Chex, milk, banana
8. Muffin, yogurt, raisins
9. Toast, milk, apricots
10. Bagel, cream cheese, juice

Lunches They Will Eat

Again, I cannot stress enough that simplicity is the key to happy mealtimes. If you haven't incorporated the acronym KISS (keep it simple sweetie) into your life, it's high time you did. By noon and following a lively recess, I found the children usually had healthy appetites. Therefore, I wanted to offer them a filling lunch, but also something they would actually consume.

The nutritional formula for lunch includes at least one serving of a grain product, a fruit or vegetable product, a dairy product, and a protein product. Sometimes I offered more than one of each of these, depending on serving sizes.

Two Weeks of Simple Lunch Ideas

1. Tuna fish sandwich, celery, apple wedges, milk
2. Cheese sandwich, tomato soup, orange slices, milk

3. Hot dogs and buns, mixed veggie sticks with dip, milk
4. Spaghetti with tomato sauce, cheese sticks, bread, peaches, milk
5. Peanut butter sandwich, carrots, bananas, milk
6. Pizza (English muffins with tomato sauce and cheese), veggie sticks, apple slices, milk
7. Chicken noodle soup, crackers, cheese sticks, orange slices, celery, milk
8. Macaroni and cheese (with real cheese), peas, peaches, milk
9. Chicken tenders, carrot sticks, bread, bananas, milk
10. Lunch meat sandwich, veggie sticks with dip, grapes, milk

Snack Time Again?

Two to three snacks a day, five times a week for a whole year equals a whole lot of crackers! Although graham crackers and milk do tend to be a favorite snack formula for young children, you may want to consider a few other options.

The nutritional formula for snacks should include two different servings from each the dairy group, the grain group, or the fruit and vegetable group. When you plan your snack menus, keep the whole day in mind. For instance, if you serve yogurt and toast for breakfast and macaroni and cheese for lunch, you probably do not want to serve crackers and cheese for a snack because you will have overloaded the grain and dairy servings and neglected the fruits and vegetables.

Some Simple Snack Ideas

1. Wheat crackers and apple juice
2. Celery and peanut butter
3. Graham crackers and milk
4. Yogurt and raisins or apple
5. Apple wedges and peanut butter
6. Crackers and cheese
7. Orange slices and cereal

8. Bananas and yogurt
9. Granola and milk
10. Carrots and popcorn*

*Popcorn and peanuts should not be served to children under three years of age due to the potential for choking.

Here are two interesting dental facts: graham crackers and raisins are two of the worst snacks for sticking to teeth and consequently promoting tooth decay. Cheese has been found to actually delay the production of mouth bacteria that can cause tooth decay.

USDA Food Subsidy Program

The U.S. Department of Agriculture currently offers a reimbursement program to assist childcare providers in serving well-balanced meals and snacks. The primary purpose behind this plan is to provide and teach proper nutrition to young children. To qualify for this subsidy, you must first become state certified with the Children's Services Division.

To attain state certification, you must first meet minimal state standards and comply with state regulations, and your home must pass health and safety inspections. Although these standards and regulations vary from state to state, if you follow this book's advice you should be well within the general legal parameters. Upon certification you can schedule a USDA adviser for an on-site visitation in your home. At that time you'll be instructed regarding nutrition, proper menu planning, meal charts, and attendance record keeping. You'll also be expected to collect parent-signed enrollment forms. The parents must be willing to receive an occasional USDA inquiry relative to their child's care and nutrition.

On a monthly basis you will be required to send in completed menus and meal attendance charts. Within a couple of months you will receive your first reimbursement check, and it should just about cover all your food expenditures. Although it entails a little extra effort on your part, it can be quite a boost to your budget. Do keep in mind, however, you will receive a W-2 form for this reimbursement at income tax time.

Some providers may prefer the autonomy of providing noncertified childcare and choose to bypass this federal money to maintain their independent status, but those interested in the USDA program should contact their state's Children's Services Division to obtain any pertinent information.

12

An Ounce of Prevention

MOST PHYSICIANS AGREE, preventive medicine is best, and the fact is, where children abound, so do germs. Be prepared to get them before they get you (the germs, that is). Now can you imagine yourself in rubber gloves and surgical mask, armed with a big can of Lysol? Look out! It's Germ Buster! You don't need to develop germ paranoia, but you will want to adopt a few basic habits and precautions.

Noses and Hands

One common daily occurrence in childcare is nose wiping. This might sound absurd, but most young children are not capable of wiping their own noses. Sure, they can take a Kleenex and smear it across their faces, but you cannot expect a young child to perform this task hygienically without some assistance. Of course, if you assess an older child as being capable, go ahead and encourage her to take care of this, but make sure she washes her hands afterward. And when you wipe children's noses, make sure *you* wash your hands as well as dispose of the used tissue. I have witnessed childcare workers use the same tissue on several children before it hit the wastebasket. They obviously do not realize that bizillions of nasty germs hide out in cute little button noses. And these same devious germs get transported from runny noses to hands to objects and finally to unsuspecting victims.

Over half of the communicable diseases could be prevented by the simple washing of hands. But unfortunately, most children do not really know *how* to wash their hands. Some think if they stick their hands in cold water for two seconds, then wipe them on their shirts, they're done. As a caregiver, you have the job to instruct. It's something you can teach as a circle time activity. You can make it into a game like a finger play and go through one step at a time. Or try replacing the words of "Row, Row, Row Your Boat" with "Wash, Wash, Wash Your Hands." Developing this one habit could help children avoid the transference of all sorts of illnesses.

The best procedure for hand washing is to vigorously scrub (medical professionals will attest, friction removes germs) using a liquid disinfectant hand soap, then rinse thoroughly in warm water. Always have paper towels available for drying. Communal cloth towels create another great germ refuge. You can purchase institutional towel holders and refill towels at many of the bulk warehouse-type stores. If you choose to use a standard paper towel bar and roll out paper towels, you may want to tear off sections (young children usually pull out too much at once).

Toileting and Diapering

You cannot expect all young children to naturally understand the correct bathroom procedure—this, too, is your job. If you care for children at the potty-training stage, you will need to fully communicate with the parents regarding their toilet-training techniques, but then you must maintain your own set of hygiene rules for the health of all the children. Hepatitis A and *E. coli* are just two of many serious diseases transmitted by improper toileting hygiene. That is another reason to keep a close eye on the bathroom throughout the day. Make certain that messes get cleaned up *as* they occur.

With Babies

When you change diapers, you have total control of the hygienic situation; therefore, it is entirely up to you to ensure sanitary standards. The basic rules for diaper changes are the following:

1. Thoroughly cleanse the child when diapering. Use disposable wipes or a washcloth that is not reused until laundered.
2. Dispose of the diaper and wipes in a sanitary manner (covered trash can).
3. Carefully disinfect the changing area after *every* diapering.
4. Thoroughly wash your hands after *every* diapering.

An inexpensive way to keep disinfectant on hand is to purchase concentrate in bulk and then dilute with water in your own spray bottle. Disinfectant works best when saturated on the surface and allowed to sit for about thirty seconds before being wiped clean. Most disinfectants are toxic to children; use them with caution. Any cleaner with the ending "sol" usually means it is a tar-based solvent and poisonous. That does not mean you cannot use it, but you must use it according to instructions, and of course, keep it out of reach of children.

Drinks and Toothbrushes

Children need to have constant access to water. The best way to provide this is with paper cups in an easy-to-use dispenser in the bathroom. Children need to drink plenty of water to avoid dehydration and also to ward off illnesses.

Some care providers like children to brush teeth after snacks and meals. Although it's a noble goal, it can be difficult to implement. You need a clearly designated and labeled space for each child's labeled toothbrush to avoid mix-ups. Tooth-brushing with many young children requires supervision to maintain sanitary standards, but it can be done. However, most dentists encourage young children to brush thoroughly twice daily. It may not be necessary or practical to provide tooth-brushing time while in childcare.

Sanitizing Other Areas

Nontoxic cleaners are available for floors, tables, chairs, cots, and cribs—places you clean frequently but do not want to overload with toxic chemicals. These, too, can be purchased in concentrate form and diluted with water in your own spray bottle.

If you care for babies or young children who put things in their mouths, you'll need to regularly disinfect toys. One quick and easy way is to keep available, yet out of the reach of children, a dishpan of a water-and-bleach solution (about one part bleach to about twenty parts water). Soak the toys for a few minutes, then allow to air dry. When the objects are completely dry, the bleach will be gone. Some plastic toys may be sturdy enough to pop in the dishwasher.

All eating utensils, plates, and cups can be disinfected in a dishwasher. If you do not have a dishwasher, you can wash and rinse dishes, then use a third rinse in water at 170 degrees. Or you can use the water-and-bleach solution (mentioned above) for the final rinse (do not use hot water; it weakens the bleach), then air dry. If you want to be really safe or are trying to prevent the latest illness from spreading, use paper plates and cups, and disposable utensils.

Just a note on sanitizing: *Never* mix your cleaning compounds. Bleach mixed or used with an ammonia product can produce lethal fumes. With any cleaning product, always remember to read the label, and store away from children. You may want to place a lock or a safety latch on your cleaning compound cupboard.

"Good Morning" Check

State-certified caregivers are required to inspect children as they arrive each morning for any health problems or signs of contagious disease. State law mandates that if the child displays certain symptoms, the caregiver must refuse admittance for that day, or as long as symptoms persist. If you choose to employ this recommended practice, include it in your written policy so parents can be forewarned. When their own children are healthy, parents appreciate this procedure—they don't want little Joey exposed to the latest bug. However, be prepared to face some agitation if parents must miss work to take their child to the doctor because you recognize some telltale signs of illness.

Making a thorough "good morning" check can be difficult as parents whirl in, disperse information, and hang up coats, while children zip off to their favorite activity. But here are some basic symptoms you need to watch out for:

- Red eyes (can be pinkeye/conjunctivitis)
- Pale skin or jaundiced (yellow) coloring
- Blotchy skin or unexplained rash
- Unexplained spots (not insect bites)
- Dull eyes
- Itchy scalp (lice; check Chapter 12)
- "Green slime" nose (the sign of an infectious cold, more than just a virus, may require antibiotics)
- Severe runny nose and fever (highly infectious cold)
- Hacking cough (might even be whooping cough, which has recently, to the surprise of many, made a comeback)

Immunizations

A state-certified center must keep records of children's up-to-date immunizations on file at all times. Most parents are familiar with this procedure and are likely to be current on their children's shots. If not, they should be. Immunizations are required when children begin public school. But they are even more important in early childhood, especially if the young child is in a group care situation and thus exposed to a high incidence of germs.

In 1993, pertussis (whooping cough) reached its all-time high since DPT (diphtheria, pertussis, tetanus) immunizations became a prominent deterrent in 1967. The Centers for Disease Control attribute this unexpected rise to the neglect of infant immunization in the last decade. Apparently, parents avoided DPT shots because of an unfounded fear of the vaccine's side effects. The statistical fact is, only one in two hundred thousand children experienced any seriously negative side effects from the DPT shots. Yet half of the unvaccinated children who contract pertussis may face hospitalization, with a one in two hundred mortality rate. These are frightening statistics, but they also make it obvious why vaccinations are good preventive medicine.

Some parents refuse immunization for their children based on religious convictions and beliefs. That need not be a great concern if you have only one child who is not immunized. Of course, that child will be at greater risk of a serious illness, but if the other children in your care are properly immunized, they should be safe from contracting any of those preventable communicable diseases. In other words, you should not have an epidemic on your hands.

Whether you are certified or not, an immunization record is a good way to be informed of the health practices of the children you care for and to be assured they are protected from certain illnesses.

A Few More Prevention Tips

- Regularly vacuum and annually steam-clean carpeted areas.
- Regularly wash hard floors.

- Maintain proper ventilation in child use area.
- Dispose of uneaten portions of food and milk products.
- Maintain proper control for insect or rodent infestations (making certain not to endanger children with toxic pesticides).
- Pets in the home must be clean and disease free.
- Maintain a "No Smoking" policy.
- Store any wet or soiled clothing in air-tight plastic bags away from children.
- Immediately launder soiled or wet bedding.
- Regularly disinfect cots or mats (this is good on a sunny day—spray and place outside to air dry).

13

A Pound
of Cure

"TEACHER, TEACHER! SHAWN threw up all over the bathroom!"

It is bound to happen. No matter how many precautions you take, children do get sick. What then?

Isolation

Before you ever begin to provide childcare, you should determine a location within your home where you could isolate a sick child if necessary, yet you want a visible place where you can still keep an eye on him. This minimizes the spread of illness to the other children while you await the sick child's parents. A cot in a nearby hallway (preferably close to a bathroom) should suffice for this temporary measure. If you haven't established an illness policy, as discussed earlier, you may end up nursing a sick child for the duration of the day. In cases where you watch only one or two children, caring for a moderately ill youngster might not be a great inconvenience, but just the same you'll need to quarantine him to prevent the sickness from spreading. No matter what your policy, always notify the child's parent in case of any illness; and remember that some diseases are so contagious you should never attempt to provide for them in a group care setting. A list of these illnesses is included at the end of this chapter.

Administering Medication

Often you'll care for children who require medication, either prescription or over-the-counter. You need permission slips readily available for parents to fill in regarding times and amounts. Then you should label the individual medicine container with the child's name and the date. Always store medication in the same designated place, *and out of reach of children*. A sealable plastic container marked "Medication" placed on a high shelf works well. You'll want a similar container for medicines that require refrigeration. This makes it easier to spot in the refrigerator, plus it separates medicine from food, preventing food contamination should a bottle of antibiotics tip over and spill.

Always double-check the prescribed dosage on the container before you dispense medicine to ensure parents have not made a mistake in the amount or times of day to be administered. If there is a notable discrepancy, check with the parents or the child's physician before giving any medicine. You should also keep a record of medication. You can use a section of your big binder organizer notebook, or simply include a little spiral notepad in your medication container. This record should list the child's name, date, medicine, dosage, and time.

Medical Release Form

State-certified centers are required to keep *medical release forms* on file at all times. This document, signed by the parent, authorizes you, the caregiver, to call for emergency medical assistance without the presence of the parent. Without this authorization, some hospitals can actually refuse treatment (if the situation is not life threatening). This form should also include the name and phone number of the child's physician, the preferred hospital, any allergies, pertinent medical information, and the parent's work and emergency phone numbers. A sample medical release form is included in Appendix A.

I kept extra copies of these completed release forms in the glove box of my van for field trips. Thank goodness, I never needed one, but it was reassuring to know they were there. Some states require these forms to be notarized. Check with your local hospital. They may have forms already made up.

Emergencies

I hope you never have a real medical emergency, but you want to be prepared and confident to handle one if it's ever necessary. The first step is to keep all emergency numbers next to your phone. Also post your address and phone number (it's surprising how flustered a person can become in an actual emergency, or it's possible someone besides you may place the call). I also kept a list with each child's name and emergency numbers next to my phone. That saves vital time in a real emergency, or once again, someone else who doesn't know where to find these numbers may place the call.

One potentially dangerous medical emergency is choking or a blocked airway; it requires instant first aid. You need to be prepared for this with young children since they have such a tendency to put things into their mouths. If you're trained in the Heimlich maneuver, apply it to the child. If you don't know it or are unsuccessful after several attempts, call 911 immediately. A blocked airway is the most serious medical emergency because survival time is so limited, but stay calm. In most communities paramedic assistance will be there within minutes. Be prepared to stay on the 911 line and follow any instructions you might receive until paramedics arrive.

Another medical emergency with young children is accidental poisoning. Although it's not as immediately threatening as a blocked airway, it can still be life threatening. If you suspect poisoning, first assess the seriousness of the situation. If it is life threatening, dial 911 immediately. If you think the child is in no immediate danger, you could call the Poison Control Center's 1–800 number (this is listed in your phone book and should also be posted by your phone). But this number is not always available, and sometimes it's not even in use. A better plan might be to call the child's physician or the local hospital, and of course, 911 could direct you to assistance even if it is not an actual emergency. Always determine the exact source of poisoning. If there's a container, keep it close at hand to read the ingredients or send along to the hospital.

Make every attempt to notify parents or their designated emergency phone number immediately or as soon as the emergency is safely under control.

Other injuries requiring emergency medical aid are usually the results of falls or other accidents. To assess the urgency of these situations, check for these signs:

- Breathing, if impaired, call 911.
- Bleeding, if uncontrollable (main arterial), call 911.
- Severe impact or trauma (did the child fall from a height or just stumble?), assess and call 911.
- Shock or loss of consciousness, call 911.

If an injury seems serious, but you are just not sure, it's always better to be safe than sorry. No one will hold it against you for dialing 911 if it does not turn out to be a real emergency.

First Aid Kit

Getting first aid training before you begin to provide care is an excellent idea, but even if you don't, you can assemble a first aid kit. An air-tight plastic container works well for holding first aid supplies. Equip it with these basics: adhesive bandages of varying sizes, gauze pads, first aid adhesive tape, antibiotic cream, tweezers, small scissors, alcohol scrubs (in individual packets), tissues, and individual packaged hand wipes. Another important first aid tool is an ice pack. It can be used to reduce swelling of bumps, bruises, and even bee stings. You can make your own ice packs by soaking sponges in water and sealing them in plastic bags, then freezing. If you're in urgent need of an ice pack and don't have one on hand, a sealed plastic bag of frozen corn or peas works wonders.

If you take children on field trips, take the first aid kit along, or simply keep a second kit in your vehicle at all times.

Irritatingly Itchy "Emergencies"

Some predicaments occur that, though nonserious in nature, are nonetheless exasperating. An occurrence of head lice is one of them. Unfortunately, it can strike even the cleanest childcare facility. If you ever notice a child repeatedly scratching her head, give it your full attention ASAP. The sooner you detect a case of head lice, the better. Perform a careful head check by following these steps:

1. Get into a bright light (outside at recess is a good time to examine heads).
2. Start by looking around the nape of the neck, around the ears, and on the crown.
3. Look for actual nits (lice eggs) on the hair shafts. They are tiny and light colored. They stick tightly to individual hairs, usually close to the scalp (a mature louse is smaller than a flea, light colored, and almost impossible to spot).
4. Watch for red irritated areas on skin or scalp.
5. Wash hands thoroughly between checking children.

If you discover a case of lice (this means nits on the hair), immediately remove the child and all her belongings from the group. Be discreet and sensitive to her feelings. It's not the child's fault. Contact the parent to pick up the child, and thoroughly check the other children.

Once you have checked all children (and with luck, it'll be an isolated case), you can then sanitize the childcare area. First, remove all soft items (dress-up clothes, pillows, area rugs, dolls, etc.) To eliminate lice or nits, you can either launder these items, put them in a freezing climate for forty-eight hours, place them in a hot dryer for thirty minutes, or remove and store away from human hosts for two weeks. Fill large trash bags with the items and store them in a garage, for example.

For the lice-infected child, you must require the parent to follow all these lice-eliminating procedures before the child can return to your care:

1. Purchase a lice-removing package like Rid or Nix or a doctor recommended product.
2. Remove and launder all bedding, soft items, and any clothing worn by the child in the last two weeks.
3. Thoroughly spray all nonwashable surfaces (carpets and upholstered furnishings) with a lice-killing spray, let sit thirty minutes, then thoroughly vacuum.
4. Use a lice-killing shampoo on the child and bathe the child.

This process is not fun, but it is necessary. Encourage the parent to do a thorough job the first time, so she may not have to repeat it. Remind her how important it is to use these delousing remedies with much care and to read the labels. These are highly toxic products that could hurt the child if used carelessly. She'll want to determine when and where the child came in contact with lice (friends, relatives, neighbors) and then make sure the child is not reexposed.

That same day you discover one case, you must inform all the other parents of the problem when they pick up their children. Explain to them that as soon as they get home they need to remove and launder the child's clothing, bathe the child, and shampoo the child's hair. At this point, if you have had only an isolated case, it is probably not necessary for them to use a lice-removal product, but it's advisable to launder any clothing and bedding used recently. If you have more than a single case, it is recommended that all families complete the lice-removal treatment.

After the children have gone home, you'll need to continue your treatment of the childcare area. Spray carpets and furnishings with a lice-killing spray (make sure to have adequate ventilation). Wait at least thirty minutes before you thoroughly vacuum the area. Follow the same instructions you have given your customers.

Just to be safe, you should continue to perform head checks for the next two to three weeks (lice nits take up to two weeks to hatch). Should you uncover another case, you may want to make copies of the correct procedures for eliminating lice and send one home with each family. If these instructions are followed, that should be the end of your little "epidemic."

Communicable Diseases

In group care situations there's always the risk of spreading contagious diseases. Colds and flu will come and go through the course of a year, but occasionally, a child will get a less common illness that is highly contagious. In this case the other parents should be notified so they can watch for symptoms to occur in their children. Some of these illnesses are listed below, along with their symptoms and incubation period. The incubation period is the time between the exposure to the illness and the actual outbreak of the disease. For instance, if one child at your center breaks out with chicken pox on February 1, you can start watching for others to break out around February 13, and the following few days.

Childhood Illnesses

Illness	Symptoms	Incubation
Chicken pox	Slight fever, skin eruption	13 to 17 days
Common cold	Runny nose, slight fever	1 to 5 days
German measles	Headache, fever, rash/spots	About 18 days
Hepatitis A	Fever, nausea, stomach pain	10 to 50 days
Hookworm	Eggs in feces	6 weeks or more
Impetigo	Skin lesions, boils	4 to 10 days
Measles	Fever, red eyes, spots/rash	About 2 weeks
Meningitis	Sudden fever, stiff neck, nausea	2 to 10 days
Pinkeye	Red, irritated, crusty eye(s)	24 to 72 hours
Strep throat	Fever, sore throat, fine rash	1 to 3 days
Whooping cough	Violent, uncontrolled cough	7 to 10 days

14

Partnering with Parents: Disciplining Procedure and Problem Solving

AS I MENTIONED earlier, you need a written policy that includes your discipline procedure. You may be wondering, though, what *is* my discipline procedure? Just as parents use different discipline measures, so will childcare providers. But you and the parents need to completely understand and agree upon exactly which method you will be using.

First, and just for the record, you should know which styles of discipline are not recommended for childcare providers. In the opinion of most professionals and Children's Services Division, any form of corporal or physical punishment is *not* acceptable, and that includes spanking.

You may be thinking, *sometimes children need a good spanking*. I happen to believe spanking is appropriate, once in a great while, but only with my *own* children, and that was only when they were small. In all the years I have provided childcare or taught preschool there was only one incident where I spanked a child, and I still regret it.

Four-year-old Jody had begun pulling some stunts at rest time. I had cared for Jody for some time, and she was usually a darling, but for some reason at naptime she decided to become downright ornery. This situation was difficult because I could not give time-outs at naptime, and the child was disrupting rest time for the entire group. I placed her cot in the hallway, but she still managed to make quite a racket. It was obvious she knew she had control of the situation. I spoke to her mom, and she suggested spanking Jody when it happened. (If Jody had been my own child, I probably would have paddled her already.)

A few more disrupted rest times passed, and finally, Jody stepped way over the line. She was so disruptive, none of the children could sleep. In frustration, I called her mother at work. I was ready to send Jody home, but her mother said, Go ahead and spank her. So I spanked Jody—and we both ended up in tears.

Fortunately, that was the only episode in years of caring for children that ever got to that extreme. After that, I set up a reward system for Jody. Every time she was a quiet rester she received a sticker. Soon the problem ceased altogether. Legal ramifications aside, I do not believe spanking is a very good option for a childcare provider.

Food deprivation is another extremely poor choice as a discipline measure. And it is illegal. It doesn't matter whether you remember your mother sending you to bed without supper or not. You should *never* threaten a child with, "Keep that up and you won't get any snack." Nor should you say, "If you don't eat your spinach you can't have any dessert." According to law, that can be classed as food deprivation.

Obviously, you want to refrain from anything that's even associated with *cruel and unusual punishment*. This commonly heard term, though difficult to define, would include humiliation, verbal abuse, restraining devices, solitary confinement, and the like. If you have further questions on discipline tactics, consult the Children's Services Division in your county, and they will provide you with specific legal information.

The best approach to discipline is always preventive. By embracing positive tactics and keeping children focused in constructive directions, you can avoid all those punitive pitfalls.

According to *Webster's Dictionary*, the real definition of *discipline* is "to train in mind and character, a mode of life in accordance with rules, self-control, order, and obedience." That sounds like a noble ambition, and it's not a bit negative. So to start with, you must adopt a positive attitude about discipline. Recognize your goal is to train, to teach self-control and respect for rules and order. Also recognize children learn more by example than by lecture. In this case, actions do speak louder than words. If children observe the adults in their lives practicing patience, exhibiting kindness, speaking gentle words, and so on, they will attempt to emulate those behaviors. Likewise, they will imitate anger, hostility, or antagonism. Unfortunately, those negative traits seem to come more readily to the basic human nature of a developing child.

I used a three-step formula for disciplining children. Of course, it isn't the only system, but it worked for me. And you can modify it to work for you.

The Rules

The first step is to establish a set of rules and make sure the children and parents know and understand them. Keep them posted at all times. The list need not be long. It can be as brief and concise as "Respect people and property." In fact, the shorter the better. Whenever possible, try to construct your rules with positive language. Instead of "No hitting," you might try "Be kind." The purpose behind positive phrasing is twofold: first of all, it sounds nicer, and, second, it doesn't simply ban a negative behavior—it gives a specific direction to move toward. You may also need to include some safety rules appropriate to your environment such as: "Children allowed in the kitchen only with adult supervision." But try to keep the rules simple so the children won't be overwhelmed by too many do's and don'ts.

Time-Out

Time-out is the consequence for breaking the rules. It needs to be a designated chair, bench, corner or whatever—situated away from the group, but within your view. A two-minute egg timer can be useful for timing this short incarceration. If a child gets up before the time-out is over (without a good reason), you can reset the timer.

When a child breaks the rules, I try to determine whether it was intentional or not and deal with it accordingly. For instance, Timmy wants a toy and whacks Sara over the head to acquire it. I call that intentional, and I deal with it immediately with a brief reminder of the "Be kind" rule and a short time-out. One way to communicate with a young child is to remind him that he does not like to be hit, and neither do his playmates. He needs this reminder because it's actually a stage of development for a child to realize and respect that other living beings experience pain (this stage occurs between the ages of two and three, and even later for some children). You might ask, "If Timmy isn't at this developmental phase yet, why give him a time-out?" The purpose of a time-out is to help break the pattern Timmy has initiated in using physical violence to get his way. It gives him a moment to regroup and imprint his short memory with the "Be kind" rule.

When a child unintentionally breaks the rules, it needs to be identified but dealt with differently. Say Lucy is dancing and accidentally knocks John's blocks down. John may be wailing at the top of his lungs, but you can see that Lucy did not mean to do it. Intervention is required. You can say something like, "Lucy, I know you didn't mean to knock over John's tower, but you need to be careful when you dance so you don't get in someone's space. Can you tell John you're sorry? Maybe you can help him rebuild his tower." This is also an opportune moment to teach John about forgiveness because accidents happen to everyone. The best thing for John is to forgive and move on. It's also important to reaffirm John's space and let him know you are sorry his tower got knocked over and what a nice job he was doing on it. It is amazing how easy it can be to smooth over childish disputes with the right dose of positive words and affirmations. The disputes can transform into highlights of learning how to get along and helping one another.

What about when Timmy bops another child on the head after you've already given him a time-out? Repeat the reminder of the rule, and tell him his time-out will have to be longer this time. Your purpose is to instruct and encourage good behavior, *not* to merely punish.

Rewards and Behavior Reports

Occasionally, a child will repeatedly and intentionally break the rules. Other than giving her a time-out all day, what can you do? First, ask yourself whether there is anything preventive you are neglecting. Are you expecting too much from her? Are you allowing her too much independence? What can you do to ensure her success? Can you set up play situations where she can maintain self-control? How can you assist her in creating some new patterns of positive behavior within the day? You do this by helping her *develop the habit of obeying the rules,* and then you acknowledge and praise her success. One incentive for her to develop these habits is to use a reward system. The easiest reward is praise, but you can also use stickers.

Another incentive to develop good habits is to use behavior reports. These reports allow parents to know how Timmy's day went. Although you want behavior reports to be as positive as possible, you are also trying to keep the parent informed about her child's progress or lack of it. You want to partner with the parents. You need their reinforcement and support in helping their children to get along better, and for this, communication must occur. Since it's usually busy when parents pick up their children, write out a behavior report. It can be a little note saying something like, "Timmy was helpful at snack time and took a good nap. But Timmy needs to work on sharing a little more." By starting the note with something positive, you give the parents hope and set the tone for them to talk positively about learning to share. You do not need to go into the details of how he hogged all the crayons or stole Sally's doll and made her cry. It will be much easier for them to talk with you if you don't lay a guilt trip on them for having such a selfish son.

When Disagreements Occur

It is bound to happen. A few weeks after you're in business, you think everything is going just swell, and boom, the honeymoon is over. It happens in various ways. Maybe one child is really a handful, or maybe a grumpy parent is making your life miserable. What can you do? These situations require tact, assertiveness, and good communication skills. First, remember that life never goes smoothly, and it's best to be prepared. Next, identify the problem. Is it an uncontrollable child? Have you really tried everything? Have you prayed for the child? Do you honestly believe this child should not be in your care?

If you're at your wit's end, you need to explain your problem gently to the parent. After all, this is your business. Furthermore, it is your home, and you must maintain control. Very likely, the parent will be more than willing to work with you to ensure the child develops self-control. If the parent is unwilling to help, you have the right to give him two weeks' notice, as spelled out in your policy. (Remember your policy?) You might wish to make yourself aware of other facilities better equipped to deal with a difficult child, in order to recommend them to the parent.

What if a parent doesn't like something you are doing? You need to ask her to specifically explain what bothers her. Do not settle for a generalization like, "I just don't like how you do things here." If she can clearly define what is wrong, you must determine whether it's a legitimate complaint and whether you can (or want to) change it. If it's an unresolvable difference, and you honestly do not believe you're at fault, remind her that she signed a policy stating she will give two weeks' notice before removing her child or else risk losing two weeks' prepaid tuition. This gives you time to fill the vacancy, and she gets time to look for another center.

In reality, these troubles are usually few and far between, but having your written policy will help immensely to deal with any problems that may occur.

Planning Your Discipline Policy

1 Make and post a list of rules.

2 Give parents a copy of these rules and your discipline policy (you may want a signed agreement with them).

3 Your policy should clearly state punitive measures you will not employ.

4 Your policy should clearly state the discipline plan you will employ (time-out, behavior reports, rewards).

5 Your policy should include a statement on your basic philosophy regarding discipline and the environment you are striving to create in your childcare business.

15

Recognizing

Special

Needs

SPECIAL NEEDS IS the current terminology for describing what, at one time, might have been called *abnormalities of childhood*. However, anyone who works with children or has children should appreciate the fact that there is really no such thing as a *normal* child. In fact, everyone has some form of special needs. Think about the adults you know. Are any two alike? Do you really know anyone who is completely *normal?*

Every child grows and develops at a different rate. What's normal for one child isn't likely to be the same for the next. Children's unique personalities, temperaments, or genetic predispositions can account for what we might mistakenly label abnormal. With this firmly in mind, we can attempt to learn how to recognize symptoms of what may actually be a problem in the development of a child, or what child development professionals call *special needs*.

No one expects you to be a medical expert or a child psychologist, but since you will probably spend more waking hours with the children you care for than their parents, you'll also be expected to observe signs of trouble. You may notice something as simple as a rash, or something much more serious such as an injury consistent with child abuse. You don't need to get out your magnifying glass to search for problems. Just use your eyes, your ears, and your brain. If something out of the ordinary catches your attention, make a dated note of it, and slip it in the child's file, such as "Jenny got a stomachache after eating chocolate birthday cake." Then if the incident repeats itself, you can mention it to the parent, who can be on the lookout for a possible intolerance to an ingredient in chocolate cake.

Allergies and Asthma

Allergic reactions usually result in hives, rashes, itching, sneezing, runny nose, or difficulty in breathing. But they can also reveal themselves in behaviors like fussiness, irritation, acting out, and such. Allergies are caused by allergens found in pollen, dust, animal hair, mold, food, and a variety of other things. About one out of five children will be affected by some form of allergy at some time in life, and allergies tend to run in families. It may help an allergy-prone child to see a specialist. Patch tests can reveal the items he is reacting to. In the meantime as a caregiver, you can make certain your home is relatively dust-free, and observe the foods, pets, plants, or whatever the child may be exposed to.

A constant occurrence of allergies can result in asthma. Asthma symptoms are shortness of breath, wheezing, and coughing. If you have an allergy-prone child in your care, you would be wise to advise she see an allergy specialist before asthma develops. If the family has an asthma history, the child will likely be affected as well. An asthma attack can be frightening for both child and caregiver. If you care for an asthmatic child, make certain you understand how to administer treatment properly.

Learning Disorders

One of the more common problems in childhood is what we term *learning disorders*, such as dyslexia, attention deficit disorder, hyperactivity, communication disorder, and minimal brain damage. This chapter cannot begin to explain all of these disorders, but it can help you learn to understand these problems and recognize some of the symptoms.

Experts now estimate that as many as 20 percent of schoolchildren experience some form of a learning disorder, although most have no noticeable disability. These disabilities are usually the result of disorders of the central nervous system, and can interfere with the way the brain receives and transmits messages. For instance, a child may appear to have visual problems, exhibited by inability to judge depth, distance, or size, and yet the eyesight checks out okay. The problem may lie in the way the brain functions, how it collects and processes information. Another symptom can be the consistent inability to sort and classify. For instance, a child continually confuses sizes, shapes, matching, and such. This could be an early sign of dyslexia, a common disorder where messages are scrambled (mixed or reversed) in the brain. However, dyslexia is usually difficult to spot in a preschooler.

ADD and ADHD

Lately we've heard a lot about ADD (attention deficit disorder) and ADHD (attention deficit/hyperactivity disorder). In early childhood, the symptoms of these disorders are more difficult to pinpoint because it's natural for young children to have a very short attention span and to be quite active. However, a child who never seems to focus, appears agitated and anxious, or is always in motion (almost as if she has been given stimulants) may be experiencing a hyperactivity disorder.

Some experts have begun diagnosing and treating ADHD in the preschool years using low doses of Ritalin. No one wants to see a child unnecessarily put on drugs just because he's acting hyper. But there's a built-in safety barrier in prescribing Ritalin because the reaction to the drug is in itself almost a part of the diagnosis. This particular drug overstimulates a "normal" person, but for a child experiencing ADHD, it calms him and helps him to focus.

Early diagnosis and treatment assist the child who can create learning habits in early childhood that will carry over into grade school. Also, early treatment protects a child's self-esteem, because an "out-of-control" kid tends to get into trouble. This is not to imply that every active or difficult child has ADHD; many are simply just that way.

Some children with hyperactivity disorder also experience attention deficit disorder, although that is not the rule. Attention deficit is harder to recognize, but it does have a few telltale symptoms. For instance, a child may seem unreasonably impulsive—never thinking before he acts. He may appear overly stimulated by noise, lights, or activity, or he may cover his ears, act out, or retreat to a corner. He may also have difficulty learning in a group situation, becoming distracted by other children's movements and sounds to the point he cannot focus his attention. However, given a quiet, undisturbed atmosphere he may be able to focus for short periods of time.

ADD is not usually recognized until school age, but if you continually notice these symptoms in a preschooler, advise parents to read up and become prepared—just in case. Many ADD children struggle through school for years before diagnosis or treatment. This can impair a child's self-esteem greatly. Treatment for ADD is similar to that for ADHD.

Understanding Learning Disorders

One way to begin to understand these disorders is to imagine an electronic device where some wires aren't connected exactly right. The machine works, but sometimes mixed messages are sent. Often a child has a learning disorder in only one area and can be "normal" in other areas.

Learning disorders can range from mild to severe. Though

no one knows for certain what causes them, there are many theories. Some experts believe brain damage occurs during pregnancy, caused by rubella, the RH factor, poor nutrition, drug abuse, fetal alcohol syndrome, smoking, accidents, or premature labor. Another theory is that brain injuries occur during the birth process, and most subject are firstborns, males, larger babies, premature babies, and infants who experience rapid or very difficult labors. Other postnatal causes of learning disorders are head injuries, poisoning, disease, prolonged nutritional deprivation, and/or abuse.

Hearing and Vision

Although hearing and vision impairments would seem the most obvious, they are often overlooked in early childhood. A child cannot tell you if she is impaired because all she knows is how she sees and hears. To her that is normal. If a child seems physically uncoordinated or clumsy, if she squints or has to get very close to see things, she may be experiencing a vision problem. The child's pediatrician can test vision and diagnose any problems.

If a child consistently doesn't follow directions or doesn't interact with other children well, you may want to check his hearing. Stand behind the child and ask him a question in a soft tone of voice (try it with, and without, background noise). You can make it into a game and do it with other children as well. That way the child does not feel self-conscious. If you sense he is not hearing you completely or correctly, you may suggest the parents have him professionally tested.

Mental Retardation

Mental retardation limits a child's ability to learn and her capacity to put learning to use. Estimates are that one in thirty-five Americans has some degree of mental retardation, although most experience only mild or moderate forms. Mental retardation is a lifelong condition that usually occurs at, or near, birth, and it is almost always recognizable by school age. It can be treated through education and therapy, but it is never "cured." Mental retardation crosses all cultural and economic borders, and is known to have multiple causes. Basically, any condition (genetic, illness, injury, etc.) that interferes with mental development before, during, or after birth can cause it.

About 90 percent of all mentally retarded persons fall into the mild category (an IQ of 53 to 67). Most are not diagnosed until school age, although they may be considered developmentally delayed or slow compared to their preschool-aged peers. Children in this category are usually very adaptable to a group care situation.

The next category is moderate (an IQ of 36 to 52). Moderately impaired children are usually recognizable in their preschool years. They have fair motor development but are often speech delayed. They need extra help in caring for their basic needs (eating, dressing, toileting) but with minimal effort can fit into a group care situation.

Severe or profound forms of retardation affect less than 5 percent of all retarded persons. They range from having some communication skills to almost none, and they often have physical disabilities as well. Children in this last group would be the most difficult to blend into a group care situation because they need so much individual care and assistance, but if the caregiver is experienced and capable, and only caring for a few children, it may be a challenge worth pursuing.

Preschool age is a wonderful time to allow small children to become comfortable with a special needs child. It is the perfect time to learn tolerance for differences. Not only that, but most young children love helping out, and a special needs child usually welcomes help.

Abuse

Probably one of the most widely discussed problems in childhood recently has been abuse. There are many forms of abuse, and each has its own identifiable symptoms (although some may overlap). As a childcare provider, you must be prepared to recognize and report suspected abuse.

Physical abuse is usually the easiest to spot because the signs are often, although not always, visible. If you notice bruises, welts, burns, cuts, broken bones, sprains, or bites, you need to ask the child how the injuries occurred and how the injuries were treated. Make a dated note describing the injury and the child's explanation of how it occurred (try to quote the child word for word when possible). If the child's explanation does not match the injury (for instance, he has deep welts across the back of his legs, but says he fell out of bed), you might suspect he has been instructed to hide the fact that physical abuse is taking place.

Neglect is failure by the parent to provide food, shelter, or medicine to a child. Or the parent leaves a child alone and unsupervised. Symptoms of neglect show up in children who *do not* want to go home with their parents, who are constantly tired or display unmet emotional, physical, or medical needs. They may be excessively clingy, emotionally demanding, or withdrawn. The key is to get them to talk about what they do at home. Ask them what they had for dinner or where they sleep at night. Keep your questions simple, and do not attempt to lead them in answering. The difference between reality and fantasy is still a little blurry for a young child. Make notes of the anwers, and see if any patterns develop.

Mental injury or threat of harm is the result of the *continuing* pattern of rejecting, ignoring, terrorizing, threatening, isolating, or corrupting a child. These children may show signs of speech or sleep disorders, may fail to grow normally, can be very aggressive or withdrawn, or show an abnormal need for emotional support.

Sexual abuse or exploitation involves *any* sexual contact with a child. It can be anything from involvement in pornography to rape. These symptoms can be similar to the ones described for mental injury. They can also be revealed in an inappropriate interest in, knowledge of, or acting out of sexual matters. Physical evidence can be observed by a child's difficulty in walking or sitting, pain or itching in the genital area, or torn, stained, or bloody underclothing.

I hope you never encounter any of these heartbreaking forms of mistreatment, but if you truly suspect abuse, you are legally required to report it to your Children's Services Division or a law enforcement agency. In most states your name will be kept confidential if you report a reasonable suspicion (in some states, however, a court of law can order the reporter's name released).

You may first wish to ask the parent about the child's symptoms. The parent's reaction can further guide you. Does he seem defensive or hostile? Do she appear more concerned with her image than with the welfare of her child? Does he deny the possibility of abuse? A "yes" answer to these questions is another reason to suspect abuse.

An innocent parent's reaction should be immediate concern, shock, and anxiety for the child's well-being. If the parent is *not* the perpetrator, she will likely want your assistance in investigating, documenting, and reporting the offense. If he does not want your help or appears as if he wants everything swept under the rug, you need to take swift action. More than half the children rescued from these situations are referred by mandatory reporters (care providers or school personnel). You may be the child's best hope in a desperate situation.

Volumes have been written on the various problems associated with child development, and as a childcare provider, you cannot be expected to be well versed in all. Many providers, because of their specific situation, will choose to familiarize themselves with a certain problem that has arisen. This is part of the coparenting role a good provider plays in the lives of the families they're involved with. By addressing these more common problems in childhood, you will begin to see how important your assessment skills are to ensure the best care for the children you nurture in your home.

16

A Final
Note

ONE MORNING, IN the midst of a roomful of active little people, it occurred to me—I'd been directly involved with young children for quite a number of years. I mentally added it up, starting with my college training, teaching overseas, my work in various preschools and childcare centers, my own sons' early childhoods, and finally the operation of my childcare facility. It amounted to nearly twenty years or nearly my entire adult life. I was astounded. And though I truly love young children, I wasn't sure I wanted to spend the next twenty years of my life singing, "Where Is Thumbkin?" with my darling little friends.

Up until this day, my family and I had made a year-by-year decision about whether we would continue to offer childcare as a home business. We discovered a certain freedom in making it a single-year commitment. It prevented that trapped feeling—as if the job had no end. It also imparted a sense of control, and that's an important aspect of operating your own business. But finally, as we tried to project for our upcoming year, we detected we'd come to a crossroads in our lives.

We'd housed the childcare business in our home for a number of years, starting out with *family childcare* and moving on to *group home care*. We'd been filled to capacity (with a waiting list). We'd had a wonderful group of children and parents. They were like family. But our boys were older, and our needs were changing. We wanted to place our house for sale and possibly build a new home (my husband's dream). At last we decided—we'd reached the end of an era.

It was early spring when I broke the news to the parents. I told them by the end of the school year I would be closing my doors to childcare. It was really quite sad, and some of us even cried (understandable since we'd been partnering in a very significant portion of their lives). Fortunately, I had some good recommendations for other childcare options (I'd been able to help other providers start childcare businesses and was glad to send business their way). It wasn't an easy decision, and though I knew my family had to come first, I still felt guilty "turning out" the families who'd come to depend on me.

In fact, the following fall while our house-building/selling plans were still in transition, two moms came over and pleaded with me to consider continuing to care for their two children, who were cousins and got along like brother and sister. I told them if I did care for the two, it would be very low-key because I planned to pursue some writing (my life goal). And I couldn't guarantee I'd be able to care for them more than a few months in advance if our house sold. They happily agreed, and I took in their two little ones. I treated the two like my own. We had fun and I still managed to get a fair amount of writing done. We truly had a delightful year.

My point is, when you choose to provide childcare in your home, *you* are in charge. *You* call the shots, keeping your priorities foremost, while offering first-rate care. For instance, if your family doesn't adjust well to a house full of children, maybe you'll want to scale down. Remember, providing childcare doesn't have to be a lifetime commitment. Often it's a temporary measure that allows a mom to stay home with her children, and yet generate some extra income. I don't know too many people who've made a lengthy career in the childcare business. Quite frankly, most people experience burnout after a number of years. But that, in no way, means you have failed. It only means you're ready to move on in your life.

As I look back over my years of caring for young children, I have a deep sense of satisfaction. I know I provided many children with a safe and loving environment that was the next best thing to being home with mom. I know many parents went to work with one less worry, one less guilt trip, because they knew their children would be well cared for. It may be a small thing, but in a way I believe I gave something back to society by ensuring a healthy, wholesome early childhood for all those children who inhabited my home for several years.

It's my hope that this book will inspire you to do likewise. I also hope I've helped elevate your opinion of the significance of childcare and encouraged you to strive for excellence in the nurturing of young children. You *can* make a difference. Or as it says in Zechariah 4:10 (excuse my loose paraphrase), "Do not despise small beginnings, for God is glad to see the work has been begun."

In closing, I want to wish you good luck and share a poem I wrote after a walk with my two charges during my final year of childcare.

Wonder Times

We walk together—separately
　　Two little ones and I
Across the road and down the path
　　Where field touches sky
Two little heads bob to and fro
　　Up and down the trail
Stopping, squatting, leaping high
　　Their energy won't fail
A worm can captivate them
　　As he squiggles on his way

Or the golden mustard blooms
  That just appeared today
They always find fulfillment
  In things which seem so small
That other kids lose sight of
  When we grow to be tall

Appendix A:

Forms

Hours and Fees Policy (Sample)

Countryside Childcare is open Monday through Friday from 7:30 A.M. until 6:00 P.M. A tardy fee will be charged for picking up your child after 6:00 P.M. ($2 for every five minutes).

We will be closed New Year's Day, Memorial Day, July 4, Labor Day, Thanksgiving, and Christmas. We also reserve the right to close if written notice is given two weeks in advance.

Tuition fees are as follows:

Monthly full-time (thirty hours or more a week)	$350
Monthly part-time (less than thirty hours a week)	$275
Hourly rate (must be paid daily)	$ 3

Tuition must be paid one month in advance unless previously arranged. A late fee of $25 will be added if tuition is more than three days overdue. The child's space will not be reserved if tuition is one week past due, and care may be terminated at that time.

If a child is ill for more than three consecutive days, the following days *(up to five more days)* will be credited to the next month's tuition. If the child misses more than two weeks (without prearrangement), his or her space may be filled by another child.

I understand the above policy, and I agree to these standards.

_____ *(signature)* _____ *(date)*

Childcare Illness Policy (Sample)

When children arrive for care, they must be in good health and free from symptoms of contagious disease or, according to state law, they must be refused admittance.

Symptoms of contagious disease can be, but are not limited to: earache, running nose, irritability, vomiting, swollen glands, fever, diarrhea, loss of appetite, headache, rash, cough, sore throat, red or running eyes, or unusual drowsiness.

Children with the following symptoms will *not* be admitted for care: fever over 100 degrees present in last twenty-four hours, more than three bouts of diarrhea, undiagnosed rash, or running or pink eyes. The child must be capable of full participation.

If a child should become ill while in my care:

1. The child will be isolated in a comfortable and visible area.
2. The parent will be notified immediately to pick up the child.
3. The child *must* be picked up within two hours.

I understand this illness policy, and I agree to meet the standards as described above.

_____ *(signature)* _____ *(date)*

Childcare Discipline Policy (Sample)

There is a need for sound and positive discipline methods in caring for young children. The purpose of good discipline is to instruct and guide children into a pattern of responsible behavior. This childcare facility uses a three-part discipline method as described:

1. The rules are displayed so that both parents and children can become aware of them: *(list your rules here; the fewer the better—see the chapter on discipline).*
2. A child who intentionally and willfully breaks the above-stated rules will be reminded in a positive manner of the need to follow these rules and then will have a time-out (sitting for several minutes in a visible, designated area).
3. If a child continues to break these rules, the parent will be notified and requested to assist in reinforcing the rules.

If, after two weeks, this three-step system does not work, and the child is deemed uncontrollable by the caregiver, for the sake and safety of the other children in care, the caregiver reserves the right to give two weeks notice of termination.

I understand the discipline policy, and I agree to maintain these standards.

_____ *(signature)* _____ *(date)*

Medical Release Form (Sample)

I _____, parent or guardian of
(print name)

_____, give permission to
(child's name)

_____ to obtain emergency
(provider's name)

medical treatment for my child, if necessary, at my preferred medical

facility _____.
(hospital's name)

Child's physician _____ Phone_____

Please note any allergies, medication, or pertinent medical history:

_____

_____

_____

This document is valid from _____ to _____
(begin date)   *(end date)*

Parent's work phone _____ Emergency phone _____

Other authorized person to pick up child _____

Parent's or guardian's signature _____

(Notarization is recommended because it can be required by a medi
cal facility.)

Field Trip Permission Slip (Sample)

I grant permission for _____
(child's name)

to be transported by _____
(provider's name)

on a field trip to _____
(destination)

on this date _____.
(date of trip)

I understand the caregiver takes every precaution to ensure my child's safety, but accidents can happen, and I will not hold the caregiver responsible should an accident occur during the transport of my child.

_____ *(signature)* _____ *(date)*

Medication Permission (Sample)

Please give my child, _____,
(child's name)

this amount _____
(how much)

of this medication _____
(name of medicine)

prescribed for _____ at _____.
(reason for medicine)   *(time of day)*

Date _____

Parent's signature _____

Daily Sign-in Sheet (Sample)

Dates from _____ to _____

_____

Child's Name	Mon.	Tues.	Wed.	Thurs.	Fri.
	Times (in/out)	(in/out)	(in/out)	(in/out)	(in/out)

Enrollment Form (Sample)

Child's name _____ Nickname _____

Child's birth date _____ Age (at entry) _____

Parents' names _____

Address _____ Phone _____

Mom's place of work _____ Phone _____

Dad's place of work _____ Phone _____

Emergency (if parent cannot be reached) phone _____

Emergency person name/relation _____

Person (other than parent) authorized to pick up child _____

_____

Doctor's name _____ Phone _____

Dentist's name _____ Phone _____

Please list/describe any of the following:

Siblings _____

Important relatives _____ Pets _____

Favorite toy/game/books _____

_____

Allergies _____

Health problems _____

_____

Food likes/dislikes _____

_____

Fears _____

Personal habits (thumb-sucking, etc.) _____

_____

Toileting habits _____

Other childcare experiences _____

_____

Any other pertinent information _____

_____

_____

All above information is factual and true, and I the undersigned am
_____ legal guardian/parent.
                        (child's name)

Guardian's or parent's signature _____

Parent Information and References (Sample)

Just as you, the parent, are interested in my background and references, I, as the caregiver, am equally interested in yours.

We will partner to provide your child with the best of care, and to do this, it will help me to know you better.

Parents' names _____

Marital status _____ How long _____

Address _____ How long _____

Other adults in home (relation) _____

Other children (names/ages/schools) _____

_____

Employment:

Mother _____ How long _____

Address _____ Phone _____

Business schedule (hours) _____

Father _____ How long _____

Address _____ Phone _____

Business schedule (hours) _____

Background:

Mother's age _____ Education _____

Ethnic heritage _____ Language spoken at home _____
 (optional)

Father's age _____ Education _____

Ethnic heritage _____ Language spoken at home _____
 (optional)

Have there been any changes in family structure (e.g., divorce/death)?

_____

Additional comments _____

_____

_____

Immunizations Form

Child's name _____ Date _____

Date of birth _____

DPT   *(list child's age and date)*

1st _____ 2nd _____

3rd _____

1 booster _____ 2 booster _____

TOPV   *(list child's age and date)*

1st _____ 2nd _____

3rd _____

1 booster _____ 2 booster _____

Measles _____

Mumps _____

Rubella _____

Tuberculin test _____

Other _____

Contracted diseases _____

_____

_____

_____

Physician's name _____ Phone _____

Appendix B:

Old Favorite Finger Plays, Songs, and Rhymes

The Wheels on the Bus (Song)

The wheels on the bus go round and round, *(Rotate hands)*
Round and round, round and round.
The wheels on the bus go round and round,
All through the town.
    2nd verse: Substitute horn for wheels—beep, beep, beep.
    3rd verse: Substitute wipers for wheels—swish, swish,
      swish.
    4th verse: Substitute lights for wheels—on and off.
    Make up your own verses.

Open, Shut Them (Song or Rhyme)

Open, shut them. Open, shut them. *(Open and shut hands)*
Give a little clap. *(Clap hands)*
Open, shut them. Open, shut them.
Lay them in your lap.
Creep them, creep them, slowly upward *(Crawl fingers)*
To your rosy cheeks. *(Hands on face)*
Open wide your shiny eyes, *(Hands cover eyes)*
And through your fingers peek. *(Peek between fingers)*

Five Little Ducks

Five little ducks went out to play *(Hold five fingers)*
Over the hill and far away. *(Move fingers up "over hill")*
Mother Duck called, Quack, quack, quack, quack.
    (Clap with quack)

Four little ducks came running back. *(Show only four fingers)*
Four little ducks went out to play. *(Hold four fingers)*
(Repeat this verse same as above with only four, then three, then
   two, then one)

(Last verse)
No little ducks went out to play *(Hold fist; sing slowly, sadly)*
Over the hill and far away.
Father Duck called, QUACK, QUACK, QUACK, QUACK! *(Loudly)*
Five little ducks came waddling back.

Itsy-Bitsy Spider (Song)

Itsy-bitsy spider climbed up the water spout.
Down came the rain and washed the spider out.
Out came the sun and dried up all the rain
And the itsy-bitsy spider crawled up the spout again.

I Had a Little Turtle (Rhyme)

I had a little turtle *(Make fist into turtle)*
He had a little box *(Put turtle fist inside other hand)*
He swam in the puddles *(Swim fist)*
He climbed on the rocks *(Climb fist up shoulder)*
He snapped at a mosquito *(Snap fingers)*
He snapped at a flea *(Snap fingers)*
He snapped at a dragonfly *(Snap fingers)*
And he snapped at me *(Snap fingers)*
He caught the mosquito *(Clap)*
He caught the flea *(Clap)*
He caught the dragonfly *(Clap)*
But he didn't catch me *(Wave finger)*

Five Little Monkeys

Five little monkeys, jumping on the bed. *(Five fingers up and down)*
One fell off and broke his head. *(One finger)*
Mama called the doctor and the doctor said, *(Dial, hold "phone")*
"No more monkeys jumping on the bed." *(Shake finger)*

(*Do rhyme with four, three, two, one monkey until the doctor says,* "NO MORE MONKEYS JUMPING ON THE BED" [*loudly*].)

Safety Rhyme

Stop *(Hold hand like traffic cop "stop")*
Look *(Hold hand like visor above eyes)*
And listen *(Cup hand to ear)*
Before you cross the street
Use your eyes *(Point to eyes)*
Use your ears *(Point to ears)*
Before you cross the street *(Walk fingers)*

Blackbirds

Two little blackbirds
Sitting on the hill *(Hold two thumbs up)*
One named Jack *(Wiggle one thumb)*
One named Jill *(Wiggle other thumb)*
Fly away Jack *(Fly one thumb away behind back)*
Fly away Jill *(Fly other thumb behind back)*
Come back Jack *(Bring one thumb back)*
Come back Jill *(Bring other thumb back)*

Teapot Song

I'm a little teapot, short and stout *(Stand; arms make circle)*
Here is my handle *(One hand on hip)*
Here is my spout *(One hand extended)*
When I get all steamed up *(Wiggle)* hear me shout,
Tip me over and pour me out! *(Tip to one side)*

Where Is Thumbkin?

Where is Thumbkin, where is Thumbkin? *(Show one thumb)*
Here I am, here I am. *(Bring out other thumb)*
"How are you today, sir?" *(Wiggle one thumb)*
"Very well, I say, sir." *(Wiggle other thumb)*
Run away. *(Put thumb behind back)*
Run away. *(Put other thumb behind back)*

(Replace Thumbkin with Pointer, Tall Man, Ringman, Pinky, by alternating fingers)

Finger Song

Put your finger in the air, in the air
Put your finger in the air, in the air
Put your finger in the air, Tell me how's the air up there?
Put your finger in the air, in the air.

> 2nd chorus: Put your finger on your head . . . Tell me is it green or red?
>
> 3rd chorus: Put your finger on your nose . . . Is that where cold wind blows?
>
> 4th chorus: Put your finger on your belly . . . Does it shake like a bowl of jelly?
>
> 5th chorus: Put your finger on your chest . . . Give it just a little rest.

If You Are Happy and You Know It

If you're happy and you know it, clap your hands *(Clap twice)*
If you're happy and you know it, clap your hands *(Clap twice)*
If you're happy and you know it
Then your face will surely show it
If you're happy and you know it, clap your hands *(Clap twice)*

> 2nd chorus: If you're happy . . . stomp your feet . . .
>
> 3rd chorus: If you're happy . . . nod your head . . .
>
> 4th chorus: If you're happy . . . shout "Amen!"

The Wise Man Built His House upon the Rock

The foolish man built his house upon the sand *(Hands hammer)*
(Repeat verse twice)
And the rains came a' tumbling down *(Rain motion with fingers)*
The rains came down and the floods came up *(Hands up and down)*
(Repeat verse twice)
And the house on the sand went smack! *(Clap loudly)*
The wise man built his house upon the rock *(Repeat twice)*
And the rains came a' tumbling down

The rains came down and the floods came up *(Repeat twice)*
But the house on the rock stood firm *(Fist upon fist)*
So build your life on the Lord Jesus Christ *(Repeat twice)*
And you will never, never, never go smack! *(Clap loudly)*

Noah Pounds with One Hammer
(Good Loud Action Song)

(You can begin by telling a little about Noah and the ark)
Noah pounds with one hammer, one hammer, one hammer
(Pound one fist on knee in hammer motion)
Noah pounds with one hammer, this fine day.
    2nd chorus: Noah pounds with two hammers . . .
      (Pound two fists on both knees)
    3rd chorus: Noah . . . three hammers *(Pound two fists,*
      one foot)
    4th chorus: Noah . . . four hammers *(Pound both fists*
      and feet)
    5th chorus: Noah . . . five hammers *(Pound fists, feet,*
      and head)
    6th chorus: Noah goes to sleep now, sleep now, sleep
      now / Noah goes to sleep now, this fine day. *(Sung in*
      a whisper, hands folded under cheek)

("Shhh." Have children pause quietly. Then in deep voice, leader says, "Then God said, 'Noah, it is time to get back to work on that ark.'" Repeat 5th chorus, loudly.)

High Stepping Horses
(Good Outside Activity)

High stepping horses, High stepping horses *(Prance)*
High stepping horses—go clippity-clippity-clop
    2nd verse: Low stepping horses . . .
    3rd verse: Fast stepping horses . . .
    4th verse: Slow stepping horses . . .

Appendix C:
Curriculum
Ideas

If you decide to offer more enrichment in your daily schedule, you may need some extra curriculum ideas to propel you along. One theme to build your curriculum upon is the seasons and holidays. This solution to planning is already laid out for you according to the calendar year. You can carry out your themes when you choose library books, plan field trips, or select science or cooking projects and such. Having a preplanned theme-style curriculum gives you a direction to follow. It gets you through the January doldrums, and it teaches many developmental concepts you may have otherwise overlooked.

To give you an idea of how to implement these seasonal themes into learning, I've outlined a monthly plan beginning with September. I always structured my yearly theme plans around the traditional school schedule, beginning with fall.

These activities are primarily aimed toward three- to five-year-olds. Some children require more assistance, depending on their age, interest, and developmental level. Remember the purpose is to *learn*, not to produce or perform. Don't worry so much about completion; instead, focus on the enjoyment of the process.

Adapt this curriculum outline to your personal needs, deleting or adding as desired. Or simply use it as a guideline to create your own curriculum.

Another theme for designing curriculum is the alphabet. For instance, beginning with *A* week, you do projects, read stories, and so on surrounding the letter *A* (e.g., play *a*lligators, make *a*pplesauce, sing the "*A*nts Go Marching"). Then next week is *B* week (e.g., focus on the color *b*lue, make *b*ean soup, sing "I'm *B*ringing Home a *B*aby *B*umble *B*ee").

₹ SEPTEMBER ₹

September brings to mind things like school buses, apples, and autumn. Some natural themes might be *getting to know you, safety awareness/fire prevention, autumn (colorful foliage, animal behavior), harvest time, and apple day.*

Week One

Getting to Know You: Focus on children as individuals—who they are, what they look like, how they feel, their homes, pets, and so on.

Project 1: "All About Me Book"

Children create book covers by gluing wallpaper onto two pieces of 8″ x 11″ heavy paper for front and back covers. Then they use five or six 8″ x 11″ blank sheets for pages. Children can lace yarn through holes you have prepunched along the left edge to bind the book. One page can be for the child to draw himself, the next can be to draw his parents, another for siblings, the next for a pet or favorite toy, the next for his house, and the next for his name. You can write the child's name in block letters with a yellow felt-tipped pen; this creates "magic" letters. The child traces over them with a pencil or crayon. The purpose is to begin to teach him to recognize his own name—not necessarily to teach him to write. Younger children may need your help to draw pictures, or you can create templates from lightweight cardboard (the sides of empty cereal boxes) for them to trace around.

Project 2: "My Face"

Using paper plates for faces, the children glue yarn, paper scraps, and other materials to create their own faces and hair. Discuss the purpose of nose, ears, and mouth. Encourage the children to think about what color their eyes and hair are, and how we are all created unique and different from one another.

Project 3: "My Body"

Using large newsprint or butcher paper cut into sheets slightly taller than each child, trace the outlines of children's bodies as they lie on the paper. They can use crayons, felt-tipped pens, or paints to color their clothing, shoes, and face. Talk about the uses of arms, hands, feet, and knees and where they are located.

Project 4: "How I Feel"

Talk about how everyone has different feelings. Act them out at circle time (song: "If You're Happy and You Know It"). Then paste construction paper shapes on paper plates to create invertible happy/sad faces.

Project 5: Special Person of the Day (or Week)

Create a "Special Person" bulletin board. Encourage children to bring photos from home (pictures of them as babies, siblings, pets, home). Show, discuss, and display photos for all to see.

Getting to Know You Songs and Finger Plays: "The More We Are Together"; "Open, Shut Them"; "Clap, Clap, Clap Your Hands"; "Put Your Finger in the Air"; "If You're Happy and You Know It"; "Sally Has a Red Dress."

The More We Are Together

(Point to children as you go around the circle, and sing their names; sung to "Have You Ever Seen a Lassie?")

> The more we are together, together, together
> The more we are together, the happier we'll be
> There's Jimmy by Susie, and Susie by Michael
> The more we are together, the happier we'll be

There's Michael by Joey, and Joey by Noah
The more we are together, the happier we'll be . . .

Week Two

· *Safety Awareness:* Focus on safety, traffic awareness, stranger danger, 911, and more.

Project 1: Telephone (911 if your community has it)

Using one 8″ x 11″ sheet of construction paper per child, have children cut in half (you can fold in the center to make a cutting line) to make two pieces (8″ x 5½″). Attach these two with yarn (for the phone cord), then make one piece into the base by pasting on twelve 1″ squares (precut by you, unless children are handy with scissors) in the design of a phone touch pad. Then using a felt-tipped pen, you (or they) can number them according to the phone (including # sign and * sign). On the receiver section of the phone, write 911 in big numbers.

After the children have made their phones, discuss the purpose of the emergency number 911. Then let them practice pushing 911 on their phones. You may want to use an actual (disconnected) phone to let them try the real thing. Also discuss how important it is to use this number only in a real emergency, and discuss what constitutes a real emergency. Let them practice talking on the phone. Create a dialogue for them to use: "My name is Michael Jones and I have an emergency . . ." You can probably get phone stickers from your local fire/emergency stations for children to take home and place on their phones.

Project 2: Traffic Light

Using construction paper, let children cut 3″ circles in red, green, and yellow and glue them in the proper order on black construction paper to create a traffic light. Talk about the meaning of each color. Talk about how dangerous it is to cross the street (young children need a grown-up) and how they should always look both ways.

Stop, Look, and Listen

Stop, look, and listen!
Before you cross the street.
Use your eyes, use your ears,
Then you use your feet.

Project 3: School Bus

This is more just for fun, but it can be tied into traffic safety since buses become more prevalent in September. The children may have siblings who ride a bus to school. Begin by halving a yellow sheet of construction paper (5½" x 8"), then draw a corner section for children to cut out (about 1½" square) to make a bus shape. Let each child cut two pretraced 2" circles from black construction paper to make wheels. Attach the wheels with brass paper fasteners so they can turn. Teach song: "The Wheels on the Bus."

Week Three

Harvest Week: Focus on farm foods, harvest time, and nutrition; it is an excellent time to plan a visit to a farm if you live near an agricultural area.

Project 1: Apple Prints

Use smaller apples (preferably older) sliced in half to dip in red poster paint in Styrofoam meat trays and print onto construction paper. You can use thumbprints in green paint to create leaves.

Project 2: Fruit Basket

Children can cut (or tear) colored construction paper into apples, oranges, bananas, and grapes (you predraw fruit shapes). Cut wax paper into 8" circles, then cut in half to create bowl shapes, and put glue along the edges (but not across the straight top edge of the bowl). Glue the bowl to construction paper. After the glue has dried, children can slip their fruit pieces in and out of their fruit bowl.

Project 3: Fruit and Vegetable Collage

Provide home-oriented magazines (you might want to tear a pile of appropriate pictures) for children to cut out fruit and veggie pictures to paste on paper to create a colorful collage. Discuss the various types of food, how they grow, and where they come from. Teach action rhyme:

Way Up in the Apple Tree

Two big apples stared down at me
So I shook and I shook
And all those apples came tumbling down

Picked one up; took a bite
Umm, delicious!

Week Four

Autumn: Focus on fall foliage, animals preparing for winter, weather changes—choose the time if or when fall is apparent in your region.

Project 1: Leaf Collage or Rubbing

After discussing the change of summer into fall, take a nature walk and look for signs of fall, collecting leaves as you go. Bring back the leaves to glue onto construction paper to create a collage. Another option is to arrange the leaves between two sheets of wax paper and press with a hot iron (with newspaper to keep the iron from sticking to the wax paper). It makes a nice window hanging. If your leaves are not too colorful, you could make autumnal rubbings. Provide orange, yellow, gold, red, and brown crayons. Put the leaves under lightweight paper, and rub crayons lightly to expose the veins and outlines of the leaves on the paper. Teach song:

Autumn Leaves Are Falling Down
(Tune: "London Bridge")

Autumn leaves are falling down, falling down, falling down
Autumn leaves are falling down, it is fall!
Take the rake and rake them up, rake them up, rake them up
Take the rake and rake them up, in a pile!

Project 2: Autumn Trees

Using scraps of orange, yellow, red, and brown construction paper, let children tear into thumb-sized shapes for leaves. Then using black construction paper let them tear a tree trunk shape (about 2" x 5"). Paste the trunk on the lower half of blue construction paper, then add leaves, the more the better.

Project 3: Circle Squirrels

Using 8" x 11" brown construction paper, draw two lines lengthwise to make three equal-sized sections for children to cut into three strips. On one strip, remove 4" to create one shorter strip. Use one of the long strips to make a hoop (this is the squirrel's body), and staple or glue the ends. Use the shorter piece to make a smaller hoop (the squirrel's head); notch ears and fold up. Attach this head to the body with staples or glue. Next, take the remaining long strip and fringe two-thirds of it to create a bushy tail, and attach it to the lower section of the body, leaving the unnotched third showing for feet. Split the leftover 4″ piece into two strips, and attach for arms.

Squirrel Rhyme
(Finger Play)

Five little squirrels, playing in the tree
The first one said, "What do I see?"
The second one said, "An eagle in the sun."
The third one said, "Let's run, let's run."
The fourth one said, "I'm not afraid."
The fifth one said, "Let's hide in the shade."
Down swooped the eagle, in a big hurry *(Flap arms like eagle)*
And the five little squirrels, away they did scurry.

Project 4: Painted Leaves

Use a folded piece of newsprint; cut it into a half-leaf shape (with a fold in the center; see diagram). Open to see the whole leaf. Have children daub or splatter generous globs of fall-colored paint (red, orange, yellow), then fold the leaf closed again. Rub the back side to spread paint around on the insides of the leaf. Open to expose a brightly colored symmetrical leaf. These make wonderful decorations.

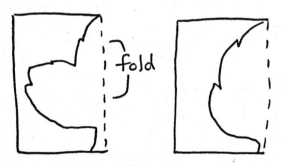

☙ OCTOBER ❧

The holiday theme this month is Columbus Day, but you can also continue to celebrate harvesttime and the change of season when animals get ready for winter and birds begin to fly south.

Weeks One and Two

Columbus Day: Focus on history, exploration, geography, and ship navigation.

Project 1: The Earth Is Round

Discuss the difference between flat and round. Use a ball and a book. Ask the children if they think the earth is round like the ball or flat like the book. Explain how people used to think the world was flat and ships would fall off the edge. Show a globe. Tell about how Columbus wanted to prove the earth was round. Give each child a blue balloon (deflated). Talk about how it is flat. Then inflate the balloons to create miniglobes, and use felt-tipped pens to carefully draw shapes that are lands. Let children trace their fingers across the blue spans (ocean) to get to the land.

Project 2: Columbus's Fleet

Use half walnut shells (you must crack nuts carefully to get even halves) for ship hulls. Put a small amount of clay inside the hull. Cut a 1″ square of paper for the sail. Insert a toothpick through the sail and into the clay as shown in the diagram. Provide a dishpan of water to sail the ships across.

Project 3: Map Making

Show children some real maps. Discuss the meaning of symbols for mountains, trees, water, and so on. Using generous sections of newsprint, children can create their own maps.

Week Four

Pumpkins and Masks: Focus on fun.

Rhymes and Songs

Five Little Pumpkins

Five little pumpkins sitting on the gate.
The first one said, "My it's getting late."
The second one said, "There are noises in the air."
The third one said, "I don't care."
The fourth one said, "Let's run, let's run."
The fifth one said, "Isn't Halloween fun!"
Then "ooooo" went the wind.
And OUT *(Clap)* went the light!
And five little pumpkins went rolling out of sight.

I'm a Little Pumpkin
(Tune: "I'm a Little Teapot")

I'm a little pumpkin, fat and round
Growing in the garden, on the ground
I'll be a jack-o'-lantern with two bright eyes
Or maybe I'll be baked into a pumpkin pie

Did You Ever See a Pumpkin?
(Tune: "Did You Ever See a Lassie")

Did you ever see a pumpkin, a pumpkin, a pumpkin?
Did you ever see a pumpkin with no face at all?
With no eyes, and no nose, and no mouth, and no teeth.
Did you ever see a pumpkin with no face at all?
So let's make a jack-o'-lantern, jack-o'-lantern,
Jack-o'-lantern, with a bright happy face.
With big eyes, and big nose, and big mouth, and big teeth,
Let's make a jack-o'-lantern with a bright happy face.

Pumpkin Story: Use a large piece of orange construction paper as you tell the story; cut the paper when shown in parentheses.

"There once was a little old woman who lived in the woods with her little cat, Toby, but they needed a new house. One day she decided to build herself and Toby a new home. She loved the color orange and decided to make her house orange (fold paper in half with fold side up like a house). Next she decided she needed her roof to slant down so the rain would run off (cut two upper corners off paper). Then she realized she had no way to enter her house. She needed a door. Since she always wore a funny old hat, she decided to make it a pointed door to accommodate her hat (cut a shape as shown below). Toby liked to go in and out of the house, and so she decided to make him his own special door with a point on top for his tail (cut a triangular shape in the center). The house was just about perfect now, except it was rather dark inside. The old woman decided she needed a window, but not just any window. She wanted a round window, shaped like the sun (cut a window on one end). Now the house was perfect, except for one thing. It was Halloween, and the old woman needed a jack-o'-lantern to place on her table (open the paper to reveal a jack-o'-lantern). Oh, that's right, she already had one!"

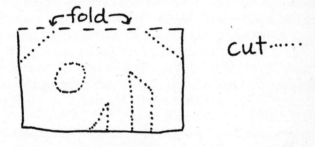

Project 1: Jack-o'-Lantern

Fold orange construction paper to cut a big circle for a pumpkin. Then cut on the fold to create a mouth and a nose (children need help with eyes). Open to show the face. Line the back of cutouts with yellow tissue paper, and make a green stem on top. Display jack-o'-lanterns on a window, and light comes through the tissue paper like a lantern.

Project 2: Paper Plate Mask

Cup two eyeholes in a paper plate. Tape a Popsicle stick to the plate for a handle. Provide various materials for children to decorate masks: yarn, lace, buttons, bright-colored paper scraps, glitter, and such.

Project 3: Pumpkin Chain

Make hoops from black and orange strips (about 4″ x 1″) of construction paper to create a paper chain. Paste small (3″) round pumpkins along the chain.

Project 4: Carve a Jack-o'-Lantern

Let children design various faces on paper, and then choose some shapes you all want to use on your pumpkin. Use a child-safe carving tool, available in craft stores, and allow children to take turns cutting the pumpkin. Let children take turns scooping out insides. Save seeds to bake later (see recipe below).

Before you place a candle inside, you might want to discuss fire safety and how only grown-ups should use matches. You might want to talk about how a light from within makes the jack-o'-lantern come to life. A jack-o'-lantern is a source of a good parable.

Recipe for Pumpkin Seeds: Rinse seeds in a bowl of water, then let them dry on a paper towel. Mix seeds with one tablespoon oil. Spread on a cookie sheet and sprinkle with salt. Bake about thirty minutes at 350 degrees. Stir occasionally until brown and crispy.

Game: Musical Pumpkins (focus on fun, not winning). Cut out one pumpkin per child (each with a different face), and arrange them on the floor in a circle with one child on each pumpkin. Play music and instruct children to walk in a circle (like musical chairs). Remove one pumpkin each time before the music stops. As children step out of the game, give them a pumpkin like a prize (so no one feels like a loser) until only one child remains.

⋲ NOVEMBER ⋲

Thanksgiving provides many curriculum possibilities from a look at the Pilgrims' *Mayflower* journey to appreciation for Native Americans. Also, it is an opportunity to focus on food, nutrition, and thankfulness.

Week One

Pilgrims: Focus on history's "olden days" when a group of people were not allowed to worship God according to their beliefs, how they knew about Columbus's discovery of a new land and decided to go.

Project 1: Shape Pilgrims

Use cutout construction paper shapes as shown below to create Pilgrims. Glue the cutouts on another piece of construction paper. Add yarn for hair. Discuss how people in "olden days" dressed.

Project 2: Mayflower

Ask children to fold brown construction paper width-wise (for the hull of a ship). With the fold on the bottom, round the edges upward to form the bow and stern, and glue along those trimmed sides to make an envelope. Create a mast by trifolding a 3″ x 13″ strip of construction paper into a stick and staple inside the middle of the hull. To the mast, attach several different size sails made of lightweight white paper.

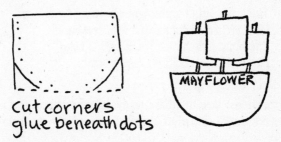

cut corners
glue beneath dots

MAYFLOWER

Project 3: Praying Hands and Bible

Children can trace and cut out hands (fingers together) from skin-colored construction paper. Next fold black construction paper width-wise and staple a sheet of white paper inside (like a book) for a Bible. Use white chalk to write the word *Bible* on the front. Attach the hands in a prayer position with a paper fastener on the cover. Inside write "God Loves Everyone." Use this project to teach the importance of religious freedom and how the Pilgrims wanted to worship God in their own way without getting imprisoned by the mean king.

Project 4: Plymouth Rock

Show on a map how far the Pilgrims traveled across the ocean, and explain how hard the journey was. Tell how thankful they were to finally reach the new country, landing on Plymouth Rock. Using one-half sheet of brown or black construction paper, have children tear off the edges to create a large rock shape. Then glue the rock to the lower left-hand corner of full-sized white construction paper. Use scraps of blue paper torn and glued to the lower left half of the paper to create the ocean. They can tear a yellow circle for the sun, small green trees to place beside the rock, or gray patches for clouds. Use no scissors (this is good for finger dexterity).

Week Two

Native Americans: Focus on how Native Americans lived, their customs and foods, and how they helped the Pilgrims. Teach this song: "One Little, Two Little, Three Little Hunters."

Rhymes and Finger Plays

The Brave Little Hunter

The brave little hunter went searching for a bear.
He searched in the forest and everywhere.
The brave little hunter found a BIG bear!
He ran like a rabbit, oh what a scare.

Project 1: Tepees

First, discuss how there are many different tribes, and they all live differently, but they had to use what was available to them where they lived. Explain how some Natives used tepees for homes. Use brown construction paper and draw a half circle (as shown). Let the children cut and then decorate their tepees with Native symbols (sun, moon, tree, etc.). Then glue the sides of the tepee together and make a slit for the door.

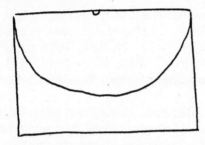 

Project 2: Wampum Beads

First, explain how the Native Americans liked to decorate using natural dyes and beading. They often used things like beads instead of coins for trading. Use various shapes of macaroni to create beads and string onto yarn. (Before this project, you can dye macaroni by putting one-eighth cup rubbing alcohol and a few drops of food coloring in a glass jar, add about one cup macaroni, and shake until color is evenly distributed. Then pour damp macaroni on a paper towel to dry. Make several colors. This method also works to color rice for collage materials.)

Another way to make beads is to cut 1″ x 3″ strips from colorful magazine pages. Then use a toothpick to tightly roll the strip, adding a small stripe of glue to hold the paper tight. (This is better for older children.)

Another way to make beads is to use craft clay and make little multicolored balls. Then poke holes in them with a toothpick. However, you should bake these when the children are not present. Keep the kitchen well-ventilated.

Beads are a wonderful way to teach sorting, counting, and eye-hand control, besides being fun.

Project 3: Native American Headdress

Using a long strip of newsprint paper about 8″ wide, fold several times to create a long sturdy strip for a headband. Let the children decorate with paints, crayons, or paper scraps. Fit to each child's head; remove and staple ends together. Predraw feather shapes onto various colored strips of construction paper for children to cut out and fringe like real feathers.

Project 4: Popcorn

Explain how the Native Americans discovered popcorn and shared it with the colonists. Draw the outline of a corn husk on brown construction paper for the children to cut out. Then children can tear kernels of corn from small scraps of yellow or orange paper and glue in even rows on the husk to create an ear of corn. Then serve popcorn for a snack.

Quick Native Fry Bread: Use biscuits that come in tubes. Fill an electric frying pan with about ½" cooking oil, and preheat to about 350 degrees. Give each child a circle of dough to pat into a patty (use flour if they're sticky), then place them in the frying pan. Keep children a safe distance from the popping oil. Brown and turn; cool and serve. You can sprinkle with cinnamon sugar.

Weeks Three and Four

More Thanksgiving Rhymes:

> Five fat turkeys are we
> We sat up all night in a tree
> When the cook came around
> We just couldn't be found
> That's why we're still here—can't you see

Five hungry Pilgrims, on Thanksgiving Day
The first one said, "I'll have corn, if I may."
The second one said, "I'll have turkey roasted."
The third one said, "I'll have cornbread toasted."
The fourth one said, "I'll have pumpkin pie."
The fifth one said, "I'll give cranberries a try."
But before they touched a single bite of turkey dressing
They all bowed their heads, for a nice Thanksgiving blessing.

> Five little turkeys sitting in a tree
> The first one said, "What's that I see?"

The second one said, "It is a man with a gun."
The third one said, "Fly away, run!"
The fourth one said, "I'm not afraid."
The fifth one said, "We can hide in the shade."
Then boom, boom, boom, went the gun!
And five little turkeys, away they did run!

The turkey is a funny bird,
His head goes wobble, wobble.
And all he says is just one word,
"Gobble, gobble, gobble."

Did You Ever See a Turkey?
(Sung to Lassie song)

Did you ever see a turkey, a turkey, a turkey?
Did you ever see a turkey on Thanksgiving Day?
Going gobble, gobble, gobble . . .
Did you ever see a turkey on Thanksgiving Day?

Turkeys and Such: Focus on food, turkeys, and a traditional Thanksgiving.

Project 1: "I Am Thankful for . . ."

First discuss how the Pilgrims barely survived their first year, and only after the Indians helped did they start to get ahead, which led to the first Thanksgiving. Use several big pieces of newsprint taped together to create a background for a community mural, writing "I Am Thankful For" across the top. Allow children to clip pictures of food or anything from magazines or draw things they are thankful for and glue them on to create a colorful mural.

Project 2: Paper Plate Turkey

Encourage children to decorate the paper plate with colorful feathers (use crayons, paint, or felt-tipped pens). Then have them cut predrawn triangles on brown paper (one 3″ body, one 2″ head) and two 1″ triangles on orange paper (feet). Assemble with glue as shown below to create turkeys.

Project 3: Edible Turkeys

Use a small orange for the body, then alternate poking cranberries and colored minimarshmallows onto toothpicks for tail feathers. Insert them into the back of the orange. Use a big marshmallow on a toothpick for the head. A cut-down Styrofoam cup makes a good prop to hold the turkey upright.

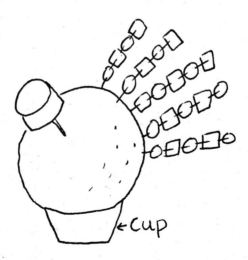

←cup

Project 4: Paper Bag Turkey

Use lunch-sized paper bags. Stuff them with wadded newspaper and tie them at the end, leaving a couple of inches for tail feathers. Have children fringe the tail feathers. Cut and glue shapes for head, feet, and wings as shown in the drawing.

Project 5: Cornucopia (Horn of Plenty)

Draw a horn shape for the children to cut from brown paper and glue edges, leaving the front open like an envelope (as shown). Then children can tear fruit shapes out of appropriate colored paper (red apples, purple grapes, etc.). These can be partially inserted into the cornucopia and glued in place to create a pleasant Thanksgiving decoration.

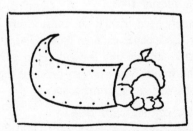

place glue beneath dots

☦ DECEMBER ☦

December is one of the most fun and busy months. There is almost an endless supply of projects and songs to go with Christmas, and it is also an appropriate time to teach about Hanukkah.

Pre-Christmas Song
(Sung to "London Bridge")

Christmas Day is coming soon, coming soon, coming soon
Christmas Day is coming soon, in the winter
Soon we'll go and get a tree, get a tree, get a tree
Soon we'll go and get a tree, in the winter
Then we'll hang our stockings up . . .
Happy Birthday, Jesus Christ . . .

Week One

Trees: Focus on trees, colors, and shapes.

Project 1: Shape Tree

Start by making a 3' triangular-shaped green tree, and attach it to a wall. Then using various-shaped 3" templates (circle, square, triangle, pentagon, hexagon, star, heart, moon, oval, etc.), help the children trace around and cut them out. They may want to decorate the shapes with colors or glitter. Discuss the different shapes and color; match and sort them according to group. Finally, attach them to the tree.

Project 2: Tissue Tree

Trace a tree-shaped triangle on construction paper. Using 1" squares of green tissue paper, children squinch little fronds to be glued onto the triangle until the tree is filled. Then glue a small brown rectangle for the trunk. (You can also decorate the tree by adding other colors of tissue paper for ornaments.)

Project 3: Scandinavian Tree

Make 1" strips of green construction paper in varying lengths of 7", 5", 3", and 1". Give each child four strips and discuss terms like *short, shorter, long,* and *longer* using these strips. Show children how to arrange the strips by lengths, long on the bottom to short on the top to create the shape of a tree, then glue to paper. Decorate with 1″ red circles. Count them out four on the bottom, three, and two. This teaches the relationship between size and number.

Project 4: Bare Trees

Discuss how winter is coming and all the deciduous trees will be leafless. Use light blue or white paper folded lengthwise, then opened up again. Put a big drop of watered-down black paint on the bottom of the paper in the fold. Show children how to gently and quickly blow the paint up the fold to create a trunk, and then spread it out (on one side only) to make branches. Quickly fold the paper closed and press both sides together to make a symmetrical print on both sides. Open to reveal the tree.

Week Two

Christmas and Hanukkah:

Hanukkah Poem

I have a little dreidel, a pretty little top
Round and round it's spinning, I'll never let it stop
Oh dreidel, pretty dreidel, My little top that spins
The children are so happy, when Hanukkah begins

Project 1: The Menorah

An important symbol for this Jewish holiday is a candelabrum with eight candles of equal height and a special lighting candle called the *shammash* separated from the rest. The eight candles symbolize when Judas Maccabaeus led the fight to regain the Jewish temple, and he needed oil to rekindle the temple light. He had enough only for one day, but the oil miraculously burned for eight days, thus the eight candles.

To create a menorah, cut lots of 3″ x 1″ white strips for candles. Then use a folded half sheet of yellow construction paper to cut the menorah as shown. Glue the candles in place. Then twist 3″ squares of orange tissue paper to create flames and glue on top of the candles.

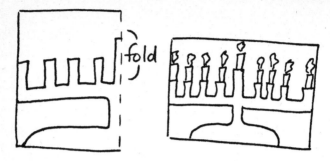

Project 2: How Many Days Till Christmas Chain

Make lots of red and green strips (4″ x 1″), and give children one for each day until Christmas. Children can alternate red and green (good patterning practice) as they construct their chains. Trace the outline of a construction paper bell about 6″ x 4″ to attach on the bottom of the chain (glitter or decorate). Then copy this little poem on the face of each bell:

> How many days till Christmas?
> It is awfully hard to tell
> Tear one link off every night
> Until you reach the bell
> Merry Christmas!

Project 3: Christmas Stockings

Make a lightweight cardboard template shaped like a stocking (about 10″ long) for children to trace onto two sheets of red construction paper. Then put the two stockings together and punch holes through both all the way around, except on top. Give children lengths of green yarn to lace their stockings together (wrap a bit of tape on one end of the yarn to make a needle). Decorate as desired. (Try writing the child's name in glue, then sprinkle with glitter.)

Project 4: Paper Plate Santa

Trim side ridges from plate as shown below, and fringe remaining ridges (for hat trim and beard). Cut leftover ridges into a mustache shape and fringe. Use two 1″ blue circles for eyes, a 2″ pink circle for the nose, and a 2″ pink circle for the mouth (mustache is glued over top half of the mouth). For hat, split red construction paper diagonally (to create two elongated triangles), glue one red triangle behind hat fringe, fold one end over, and glue a cotton ball on the tip. Children can curl beard and hat fringe with a pencil.

Week Three

More Christmas: Children love to give gifts. Listed below are some easy gift ideas.

Candle Holders: Collect enough small jars (baby food jars work well) so each child can have one or two. Use cut or torn scraps of colorful tissue paper dipped into a half-and-half mixture of glue and water and smoothed onto the jar (only one layer thick with edges overlapping). While glue is still wet, you can dip jar rim into glitter. Use votive candles.

Chip Off the Old Block: First take snapshot (or Polaroid) pictures of each child. Then you need one (2″ to 3″) block of wood per child. Children can paint their blocks with red, green, or white poster paint. After blocks dry, use Q-tips dipped in paints to decorate them (spots, squiggles, etc.). When dry, write with indelible felt-tipped pen: "Just a Chip Off the Old Block," child's name, and date. Then brush on a water-based polymer coating and adhere the picture while still wet.

Add a final coat. When dry, tie a thin ribbon around the block like a gift box.

Christmas Wreath: Save enough cereal and cracker boxes to cut out one 9″ wreath per child and paint green. After dry, glue 3″ squares of squinched green tissue paper over the entire face of the wreath. Make silver bells by covering cutout egg carton sections with foil, string them on ribbon, and tie them to the wreath. Attach a red tissue paper bow.

Macaroni Art: You can do a lot with macaroni, from covering frozen juice containers for pencil holders to jar lids for cute storage jars to picture frames (just use a precut cardboard frame with cardboard backing).

Wallpaper Booklets: Cover lightweight 8″ cardboard squares with a 12″ square of wallpaper, fold the mitred edges in, and then glue a 7″ square piece of wallpaper on the inside. Make two, one each for the front and back covers, then cut 8″ blank pages to fit inside, punch holes, and lace with matching yarn or ribbon. (See diagram below.)

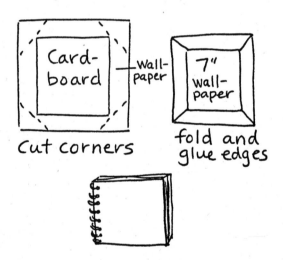

Cut corners   fold and glue edges

Stationery: Create a folder in much the same way as the wallpaper booklet, only with pockets inside. Children can use stamps or stencils or draw objects to decorate stationery and envelopes, then tuck inside the folder.

Dough Ornaments: Mix 4 cups flour, 1 cup salt, and 1½ cups water into dough, and knead. Children can shape their own ornaments (not more than 1″ thick) or use Christmas cookie cutters. Use a toothpick to make a hole to hang from or insert a paper clip. Dry twenty-four hours on wax paper, then bake for one hour on a nonstick cookie sheet (or foil) at 300 degrees. Paint. When dry, spray with an acrylic finish.

Wrapping Paper: Use sheets of newsprint or tissue paper, and stamp with vegetable prints (carrots or potatoes cut to desired shapes) using red and green poster paint in Styrofoam trays.

For tie-dye paper, use white tissue paper, folded over and over until it is about 6″ wide, then dip corners into bowls of various colored solutions of water and food coloring. Carefully open and hang to dry.

For splatter paint paper, allow children to splatter Christmas colors with brushes onto big sheets of newsprint. This requires a scrubbable area and close supervision.

A wooden laundry rack works well to dry artwork.

Favorite Christmas Songs: "Jingle Bells," "Rudolph the Red-Nosed Reindeer," "Frosty," and "Away in the Manger."

Twinkle, Twinkle Big Bright Star
(Sung to "Twinkle, Twinkle Little Star")

Twinkle, twinkle big bright star
Twinkle near and twinkle far
Wise men followed you at night
Shining big and shining bright
Twinkle, twinkle all the way
Show us where the baby lay

Ring the Bells
(Sung to "Row, Row, Row Your Boat")

Ring, ring, ring the bells
Ring them loud and clear
Tell the people everywhere
Christmas time is here
2nd verse: Clap, clap, clap your hands . . .
3rd verse: Stamp, stamp, stamp your feet .

We Wish You a Merry Christmas

We wish you a Merry Christmas
We wish you a Merry Christmas
We wish you a Merry Christmas
And a Happy New Year
    2nd verse: Let's all do a little clapping (3x)
    And spread Christmas cheer
    3rd verse: Let's all do a little dancing . . .
    And spread Christmas cheer

Rhymes and Finger Plays for Christmas

Here is the chimney *(Make fist with thumb inside)*
Here is the top *(Cup other hand over fist)*
Open it up *(Remove hand covering)*
Out Santa will pop *(Pop up thumb)*

This is Santa's workshop *(Make roof shape with both hands)*
Here is Santa Claus *(Wiggle one thumb inside)*
These are Santa's little elves *(Wiggle fingers)*
Putting toys upon the shelves

This is the stable on Christmas night *(Form roof with hands)*
High above the star shined bright *(Make fingers "twinkle")*
Down in the manger, nestled in hay *(Make cradle with arms)*
This is where baby Jesus lay

Three Kings

We three kings have come from afar *(Hold three fingers)*
Following, following yonder star *(Make hand go over hills and
    point to star)*
Frankincense, gold, and myrrh we bring *(Hold hands like cup)*
To lay before our newborn King *(Lay gifts down)*

    Five little bells hanging in a row
    The first one said, "Ring me slow."
    The second one said, "Ring me fast."

The third one said, "Ring me last."
The fourth one said, "Ring me if you may."
The fifth one said, "Ring me on Christmas Day."

Starting with the following curriculum, I will list projects and activities according to the months. You can arrange them as you like since you have now seen a sample of curriculum planning.

⚜ JANUARY ⚜

A natural focus of January can be winter. Even if you live in a more temperate climate, children love hearing about weather and snow.

Project 1: Cutout Snowflakes

The trick to make good snowflakes is to use lightweight paper, like tissue paper or tracing paper, and start with a square. Then fold and crease the paper three times. You can trace some easy-to-cut shapes in the right places on the folded paper, so the children don't cut the snowflake in the wrong spot and end up with lots of little snowflakes. These are pretty taped to windows.

Project 2: Snowmen

Allow the children to trace the outline of a snowman on construction paper (using round various-sized templates). Then they can fill in the circles with cotton balls. Collect little twigs outside to use as snowmen arms, and glue on buttons for eyes, yarn for mouth, and so on.

Project 3: Marshmallow Snowmen

Use a toothpick to stack three large marshmallows to make the snowman's body. Use two more toothpicks with tiny marshmallows to make arms. Make edible glue with powdered sugar and a pinch of water to glue on raisin eyes, and mouth. This project is especially good for small-muscle control and finger dexterity.

Project 4: Snowy Day

Use a dark-colored (dark blue or black) sheet of construction paper. Then pour thickly mixed white poster paint onto Styrofoam meat trays. Using Q-tips for paintbrushes, children can dab white spots for falling snowflakes. Then they can use their thumbprints to make snow on the ground, or to create thumbprint snowmen.

Project 5: Mittens

Trace a mitten shape around the children's hands on colored construction paper. Then they cut out the shape and decorate their mittens. You can also mark left and right and practice which is which. Use a hole punch on each mitten and attach with yarn to wear around the child's neck.

Project 6: Building a Snowman

Trace three balls on white paper in different sizes. Discuss sizes with children (small, medium, and large). Cut out balls and ask children to decide how to build the snowman (which ball goes on the bottom? which on the top?). Let them paste on paper and decorate. This project teaches size and placement concepts (i.e., big and little, top and bottom).

Project 7: Popcorn Snowstorm

Spread a sheet on the floor. Using a hot-air popper, let it shoot onto the sheet. Do not allow children to get too close (you do not want them to get burned). They can eat some and then use some to create blizzard pictures by gluing popcorn onto dark-colored paper like snow.

Project 8: Pinecone Bird Feeders

Using good-sized pinecones, perhaps gathered while on a walk, spread them with peanut butter (messy, but fun). Then allow the children to roll the pinecones in birdseed, oatmeal, or sunflower seeds. Tie a sturdy string to the top of the cone, and children can take them home to suspend from a tree for birds to enjoy.

Winter Songs and Action Rhymes:

Ten Little Mittens

(Cut ten mitten shapes, and attach them with paper clips to a string. Let two children hold the ends, while others remove mittens.)

> Ten little mittens hanging on the line
> One fell off, and then there were nine

Nine little mittens hanging nice and straight
One blew away, and then there were eight
Eight little mittens waving up to heaven
A breeze caught one, and then there were seven
Seven little mittens doing lots of tricks
A kitten took one, and then there were six
Six little mittens, see them dip and dive
A girl found one, and then there were five
Five little mittens, flapping by the door
Mother took one, and then there were four
Four little mittens, flying wild and free
One flew off, and then there were three
Three little mittens, looking bright and new
A boy snatched one, and then there were two
Two little mittens, dancing in the sun
A bird plucked one, and then there was one
One little mitten hanging all alone
Until it fell off, and then there were none

Winter Snow Is Falling Down
(Sung to "London Bridge")

Winter snow is falling down, falling down, falling down.
Winter snow is falling down, on the ground.
Take a shovel and make a path, make a path, make a path.
Take a shovel and make a path, straight and wide.

Five Little Snowmen

Five little snowmen, standing by my door
One melted away, and then there were four
Four little snowmen, climbing up a tree
One melted away, and then there were three
Three little snowmen, looking bright and new
One melted away, and then there were two
Two little snowmen, playing in the sun
One melted away, and then there was one
One little snowman, standing all alone
He melted away, and now there are none

Building a Snowman

First you make a snowball, big and fat and round
Then you take and roll it, all along the ground
Then you stack your snowballs, one and two and three
Now you have a snowman, happy as can be!
Then the sun shines bright and hot, warming all around
And your snowman slowly fades and melts into the ground

Mitten Song

Thumb in the thumb place, fingers all together
This is the song we sing in mitten weather
When it is frosty, it doesn't matter whether
Mittens are wool or made of finest leather

Winter Wear

First pull on your sweater, snug and warm, you see
Next slip on a jacket, zip it carefully
Now take a fuzzy hat and pull it over your head
Wrap a scarf around your neck, whether it's blue or red
Now slip on your mittens, first one hand, then two
Last of all rubber boots can fit right over your shoes
Now you can go out and play, in snow and cold and ice
And still be warm and comfortable, isn't that nice?

Snowman and the Bunny

A chubby little snowman, *(Make a fist)*
Has a carrot nose. *(Poke out a thumb)*
When along hops a bunny, *(Make other hand rabbit ears)*
Now what do you suppose?
This hungry little bunny,
Is looking for his lunch.
He eats the snowman's carrot nose,
Crunch! Crunch! Crunch!

Snowmen

Five little snowmen, standing in a row
Each with a hat, and a big red bow
Five little snowmen, dressed for a show
Now they are ready, but where will they go?
Wait until the sun shines, soon they will go
Down the hill, and through the field,
with the melting snow
(Start with five fingers spread, slowly shrink down into fist)

₺ FEBRUARY ₺

This month we primarily think of Valentine's Day, and yet there are some other significant days: Washington's and Lincoln's birthdays.

Project 1: Lincoln's Cabin

Use a piece of blue construction paper for the background. Let the children use a template shaped like a house to trace a cabin, then fill in the cabin by gluing on pretzel sticks horizontally like logs. Use pretzel sticks to make tree trunks and color in treetops with green crayons. Discuss how cabins were built, and how Lincoln's family was very poor.

Project 2: Heart Prints

Cut potatoes in half and carve out various-sized hearts to make stamps. Create posters by using the potato prints dipped in red and pink paint, stamped onto white paper. You can also use these stamps to make frames. Stamp along poster board cut into mat frames; then use the frame to place child's artwork inside and give for a Valentine gift.

Project 3: Heart Collage

Using red, pink, and white tissue paper, cut out a variety of hearts and spread them on the table. Mix white glue with water to a milky consistency (baby food jars work well to contain glue solution). Children can paint this mixture onto poster board or heavy paper. Then children can overlay hearts onto the wet paper to create different shapes. Then help them carefully brush on more glue solution to coat the picture.

Project 4: Heart Print

Fold butcher paper and draw a half heart. Allow children to cut out and open to see the heart shape. Then splatter red and pink paint onto the heart and fold again while wet to create a symmetric image on the heart.

Project 5: Valentine Creatures

Using various-sized construction paper hearts, attach with accordion folded arms and legs to make creatures.

Project 6: Love Beads

Using Fruit Loops-type cereal, have children string loops on yarn to create necklaces. In the center attach a pink heart that says, "I love you," to form a pendant.

Project 7: Valentine Holders

Have children cut two pretraced hearts from butcher paper (about 18" square). Punch holes around the sides and bottom of both hearts, leaving the top open. Let children lace with red yarn or paper ribbon to create a folder. Decorate with glitter, hearts, stickers, candy hearts, and lace. A fancy way to label the folder is to write the child's name with glue and sprinkle red glitter. Then hang them securely by the door on Valentine's Day for the children to fill with valentines.

Project 8: Handmade Valentines

Provide lots of materials to choose from: old valentines, buttons, lace, foil, stickers, glitter, ribbons, scraps of pink and red paper, and glue. Fold white construction paper in half to form cards and ask children to dictate their valentine messages to their parents. Then children can get creative in decorating their cards.

Project 9: George Washington's Hat

Split diagonally an 8" x 11" sheet of white construction paper. Staple two shorter sides together to form a triangular hat. Talk about how people dressed during the Revolution and how George wore a hat like that and was a general and such. Read a book about Washington.

Project 10: Betsy Ross Flag

Give each child one sheet of white construction paper, seven 1" x 11" strips of red construction paper, and a 5½" x 4" rectangle of blue. Help them to arrange the flag, and discuss how it was first created for our country. Use stick-on stars to make a circle of thirteen in the field of blue.

Project 11: Coin Rubbings

Have coins depicting Washington and Lincoln (quarters, pennies) available. Using lightweight paper and crayons or colored pencils, make rubbings of the presidents' heads to create small posters.

Project 12: George's Cherry Tree

Provide precut shapes: 2″ x 4″ brown rectangle (trunk), 6″ green circle (treetop), ½″ x 3″ black strip (hatchet handle), 1½″ x ½″ gray rectangle (hatchet head). Use a hole punch to make lots of little red circles (cherries). Tell the legend of how George supposedly cut down his father's cherry tree with his new hatchet and how he could not tell a lie. This is a good folk tale to reinforce truthfulness. Use the paper pieces like a puzzle to create the pictures. The tree can be standing or cut down. Then let the children glue them on to create a picture.

February Songs and Finger Plays

George Washington Song
(Sung to "Yankee Doodle")

Very many years ago, when our country was young
There lived a man so brave and smart, his name was Washington
On his birthday, let us sing
Sing in celebration
As we remember Washington
The father of our nation
He became a general, our armies to command
Later he was president, the first one in our land
On his birthday, let us sing . . .

Young George

When George chopped down the cherry tree
He could not tell a lie
He went to his father straight away
And said, "I'm sorry, it was I."

Five Little Valentines

Five little valentines, playing on the floor
One skipped away, and then there were four
Four little valentines, sitting in a tree
One blew away, and then there were three
Three little valentines, saying I love you
One jumped in the mailbox, and then there were two
Two little valentines, looking for some fun
One slipped out the door, and then there was one
One little valentine, feeling all alone
Hopped into my pocket, and now there are none

Valentine Song
(Sung to "Have You Ever Seen a Lassie?")

Will you be my valentine, my valentine, my valentine?
Will you be my valentine, this Valentine's Day?
I love you, I love you . . . ("this way and that way")
Oh, will you be my valentine, this Valentine's Day?

₺ MARCH ₺

March brings the beginning of spring, windy days, kites, daffodils, St. Patrick's Day, and more.

Project 1: Forsythia Branches

Using a piece of sky blue construction paper for the background, children can use brown or black crayons to draw branches. Then they can squinch little squares of yellow tissue paper for blossoms to be glued along the branches. They can use the same technique to make blossoming cherry trees, using pink tissue squares.

Project 2: March Comes in Like a Lion

Children can cut one 8″ brown circle for the lion head and attach two (2″) circles for ears. Use a triangle for the nose, two half-circles for the eyes, and thin 8″ strips for whiskers. For the lion's mane, cut many yellow and orange strips (about 3″ x 1″). Children can curl these strips around pencils or crayons and attach around the perimeter of the large circle.

Project 3: And Goes Out Like a Lamb

Make a cardboard template of a lamb for children to trace around and cut out on construction paper. Then use white cotton to glue onto lamb for wool.

Project 4: Weather Dial

March often has diverse weather, so it provides a good opportunity to learn about various weather conditions. Using a paper plate with an X drawn through to divide into quarters, allow the children to paste on various weather symbols (e.g., umbrella, sun, gray cloud, kite for wind). Then attach a black arrow in the center with brass paper holder. Children can turn the arrow to the type of weather for each day.

Project 5: Giant Daffodils

Trace the shape of a five-petaled daffodil on yellow construction paper that has a 6" diameter. For the center use a yellow cupcake paper. Cut green stems and leaves to attach to daffodils.

Project 6: Fuzzy Caterpillars

Spring is an excellent time to talk about insects. Have pom-poms available for children to glue together in a line to create caterpillars. They can be climbing branches, or crawling in the grass.

Project 7: Egg Carton Caterpillars

Separate paper egg cartons to make two strips of six. Let the children paint and decorate to create colorful caterpillars. Then use two 3" pipe cleaners to make antennas.

Project 8: Tissue Paper Butterflies

Using colorful squares of tissue paper, scrunch in the middle and twist a pipe cleaner around it to make the body and antennas. (See diagram.)

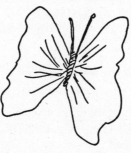

Project 9: St. Patrick's Day

Trace the shape of an 8" potato on brown construction paper for the children to cut out. Ask them to draw a face on the potato. You can mention that this is an Irish holiday, and a lot of potatoes are eaten in Ireland. Children can cut out green hats to place on top of the potatoes. Then provide lots of green 3" strips to be attached with brass fasteners as arms and legs.

Project 10: Kites

Glue or staple butcher paper (folded into a diamond kite shape) onto two strips of heavy (poster board weight) paper (cross-shaped). Children can decorate kites, make tails, and attach short strings to fly them. (See diagram.)

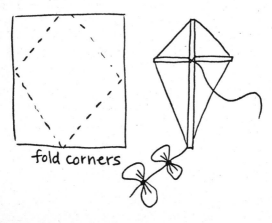

fold corners

Project 11: Pussy Willow Prints

Using gray paint and thumbprints, make pussy willows by printing thumbs on branches predrawn on paper.

Other Spring Projects: Plant marigold seeds. Grow alfalfa sprouts. Blow bubbles.

March (Spring) Songs and Finger Plays
Jack and Jill

Two little blackbirds sitting on a hill *(Hold two thumbs up)*
One named Jack and one named Jill *(Wiggle one thumb,*
   then the other)

Fly away Jack *(Flutter one hand away behind back)*
Fly away Jill *(Flutter the other hand away behind back)*
Come back Jack *(Flutter one hand back)*
Come back Jill *(Flutter the other hand back)*

My Garden

This is the way I plant my garden
Digging, digging in the ground *(Pretend to dig)*
The sun shines warm and bright above it *(Raise arms)*
Gently the rain comes falling down *(Flutter fingers)*
This is the way the small seeds open *(Slowly open fist)*
Slowly the shoots begin to grow *(Hold some fingers up)*
These are my pretty garden flowers *(Hold all fingers up)*
Standing, standing in a row

Here's a Baby Birdie
(Tune: "Tammy Is a Welsh Man")

Here's a baby birdie *(Children curl into ball)*
Hatching from his shell *(Wiggle in ball)*
Out pops his beak *(Stick head up)*
Out pops his tail
Now his legs, he stretches *(Stand up)*
His wings give a flap *(Flap arms)*
Now he flies and flies and flies *(Flutter arms)*
Now what do you think of that?
Down, down, down, down . . . *(Voice and body go down)*
Boom *(Flop to floor)*

Fuzzy Wuzzy Caterpillar

Fuzzy wuzzy caterpillar into a corner will creep
She spins herself a blanket, and then goes fast to sleep
Fuzzy wuzzy caterpillar wakes up by and by
To find colorful wings of beauty
She's turned into a butterfly

Ten Fluffy Baby Chicks

Ten fluffy baby chicks looking nice and fine
One chased a bug and then there were nine
Nine fluffy baby chicks by the garden gate
One ran away and then there were eight
Eight fluffy baby chicks looking up to heaven
One followed a butterfly and then there were seven
Seven fluffy baby chicks playing with some sticks
One went to eat a worm and then there were six
Six fluffy baby chicks by a buzzing hive
One trotted to the horse corral and then there were five
Five fluffy baby chicks by the chicken coop door
One went with the ducks to play and then there were
     four
Four fluffy baby chicks under the apple tree
One took a nap and then there were three
Three fluffy baby chicks looking for something to do
One fluttered to the pig pen and then there were two
Two fluffy baby chicks playing in the sun
One went to see the cows and then there was one
One fluffy baby chick standing all alone
He went to Mother Hen and then there were none

You Are My Sunshine

You are my sunshine, my only sunshine
You make me happy, when skies are gray
You'll never know dear, how much I love you
Please do not take my sunshine away

The Wind

Who has seen the wind?
Neither you nor I
But when the trees bow their heads
The wind is passing by

The Wind

The wind came out to sweep the sky
The fluffy clouds went flying by
The flowers danced, the grass did too
The branches waved, and the wind blew
It took my kite to the greatest height
Then the string broke and my kite took flight

₺ APRIL ₺

Easter usually falls in April; this is also a good month to continue the focus on spring, baby animals, flowers, and such.

Project 1: Baby Chicks

Shake cotton balls in a plastic bag with about a tablespoon of yellow powdered poster paint until cotton balls are yellow. Give children an 8" x 11" piece of sky blue construction paper and a green strip to make grass along the bottom (they can fringe green strip or tear edges). Also have children cut out several 3" egg shapes and then tear the eggs in two (as if they cracked open). Then use the yellow cotton balls to glue onto paper like chicks. Use orange crayon to draw legs and beaks. (See diagram.)

Project 2: April Showers

Have wallpaper book available for children to select a page. Use an umbrella-shaped template for children to trace onto wallpaper and cut out (about 6" diameter). Then trace shapes of two black boots to be cut out and pasted under a yellow triangle (for a raincoat) and beneath the umbrella. (See diagram.)

Project 3: Bunny Masks

Each child decorates a paper plate with cutout paper bunny ears, nose, whiskers, and bow tie. Cut eyeholes and attach strings to tie around the child's head.

Project 4: Eggs in a Basket

Show children how to cut a crescent shape from brown construction paper (about 8″ diameter). Put glue on the edge of the bottom half and attach to a full sheet of construction paper, leaving the top open. Draw a basket handle with a brown crayon and attach a tissue paper bow on top. Have egg-shaped templates available for tracing onto colored paper. Children can decorate them and slip them into the basket with Easter grass. They can count how many eggs in, how many out, and how many altogether. (See diagram.)

(glue beneath dots)

Project 5: Dyeing Eggs

Use three clear glass jars. Partly fill each with warm water, one teaspoon of vinegar, and several drops of food coloring in primary colors (blue, red, yellow). Talk about the colors. Explain how these three colors can make lots more. Then take turns dipping hard-boiled eggs. First dip in one color only. Next time dip in two to mix the colors to create purple, orange, and green. Talk about which colors mix to make what.

Project 6: Tulip Garden

Cut potatoes in half, and notch two Vs from the top to create tulip-shaped prints. (See diagram.) Using red, yellow, and pink paint (in meat trays), dip tulip shapes and print across upper half of construction paper. For grass cut deep Vs from potatoes to make grass shape. Dip this print into green paint and stamp along the bottom. Use green felt-tipped pens to connect tulips to grass for stems.

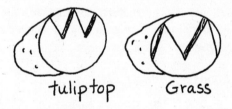

tulip top　　　　Grass

Project 7: Giant Egg

Use butcher paper to cut out giant egg shapes, and let children paint to decorate.

Project 8: Egg Prints

Cut sponges into egg shapes to dip into pastel-colored paint in meat trays, and print. You can make pastel colors by mixing white into any of the traditional colors.

Project 9: Paper Plate Duck

Cut paper plates in half. Use one half for the body; turn the other half sideways and glue on for the head. Attach orange feet and a triangle beak. Make an eye. (See diagram.)

Project 10: Easter Puzzles

Take the fronts of old Easter cards for children to glue onto poster board cut the same size (paint on diluted glue with paintbrush). After cards are thoroughly dried, help children cut cards into several different puzzle pieces. The children can enjoy reconstructing their pieces to make the picture. Give each child an envelope to keep the puzzle pieces together.

April Songs and Finger Plays

Ten Yellow Chicks

Five eggs, and five eggs _(Hold up all fingers)_
That makes ten!
Nesting on top is a Mother Hen. _(Fold arms like wings)_
"Cackle, Cackle, Cackle!"
Now what do you see?
Ten yellow chickies _(Wiggle ten fingers)_
Fluffy as can be.

Here Comes Peter Cottontail

Here comes Peter Cottontail, hopping down the bunny trail
Hippity, hoppity, Easter's on its way . . .

He brings lots of gifts and toys
To all the little girls and boys
Hippity, hoppity, soon it's Easter Day!

The Garden Song
(Sung to "Row, Row, Row Your Boat")

Plant, plant, plant your seeds
In a nice straight row
Soon you'll see some little sprouts
And watch the flowers grow
Hoe, hoe, hoe the weeds
In the garden bed
Watch the flowers blooming now
Yellow, pink, and red
Pick, pick, pick the blooms
In a big bouquet
Give them to your mother dear
What do you think she'll say?

Rainbow Song

Red and yellow and pink and green
Purple and orange and blue
I can sing a rainbow, sing a rainbow
Sing a rainbow too.

Five Pretty Easter Eggs

Five pretty Easter eggs, rolled in my door
My kitten ran away with one, and then there were four
Four pretty Easter eggs, hiding by a tree
My puppy carried one away, and then there were three
Three pretty Easter eggs, in my father's shoe
He took one to work with him, and then there were two
Two pretty Easter eggs, sitting in the sun
My sister took one to school, and then there was one
One lonely Easter egg, pretty as can be
I'll take it home for Mommy and me

Baby Animal Song
(Sung to "London Bridge")

Baby chicks go peep, peep, peep
Peep, peep, peep
Peep, peep, peep
Baby chicks go peep, peep, peep
In the barnyard
   2nd verse: Baby birds go chirp, chirp, chirp . . .
   In the treetops
   3rd verse: Baby lambs go baa, baa, baa . . .
   In the barnyard
   4th verse: Baby puppies go yip, yip, yip . . .
   In my backyard

April Showers
(Sung to "London Bridge")

April showers falling down
Falling down, falling down
April showers falling down
In the springtime

Rainy Day

Pitter patter, pitter patter
Rain is falling from the sky
But I have my umbrella
To keep me warm and dry
When the shower ends
The sun begins to glow
Pretty flowers start to bud
And grow and grow and grow

Ten Little Bunnies

One little, two little, three little bunnies
Four little, five little, six little bunnies
Seven little, eight little, nine little bunnies
Ten little bunnies, all hiding their eggs

2nd verse: We'll go out and find their eggs (3x)
All on Easter morning

The Easter Song
(Sung to "London Bridge")

Jesus died for you and me,
You and me, you and me
Jesus died for you and me, on the cross
    2nd verse: They laid him in a rich man's tomb,
    Rich man's tomb, rich man's tomb
    They laid him in a rich man's tomb and closed the door
    3rd verse: Angels rolled the stone away,
    Stone away, stone away
    Angels rolled the stone away, on that morn
    4th verse: Jesus rose up from the grave,
    From the grave, from the grave
    Jesus rose up from the grave on Easter Day!

Other Spring Projects: Grow bulbs in water. Use toothpicks to suspend bulb halfway in water. Make sure the water is filled regularly. Make a small garden in a large wooden box outside—easy-to-grow plants include carrots, lettuce, radishes, green onions, strawberries, and tomatoes. Visit a farm to see baby animals.

⚜ MAY ⚜

May is another fun spring month with a focus on May baskets, Mother's Day, and activities in the sun.

Project 1: May Baskets

Draw a half-circle shape onto a piece of construction paper lengthwise (using the long edge of the paper for the half cut of the circle). The children can cut out the half circles and decorate them with crayons, felt-tipped pens, or chalk. Then shape them into cones by either stapling or gluing the flat edges together. Use an 8" x 1" strip to attach for the handle and decorate with a bow. If you live near a field, you might take a spring walk and collect flowers for the May basket. Otherwise you could use colorful 6″ squares of tissue paper squinched into blooms and wrapped with green pipe cleaner stems to create flowers.

Project 2: Flying Bluebirds

Trace the body of a bird and wings onto blue construction paper (as shown). Children can color bluebird's breast red on both sides. Make a careful slit (as shown) and insert wings to make a 3-D bird. Attach string with needle and thread in the center of the back. Children may wish to make several and create a bluebird mobile by attaching them to a stick at varying levels.

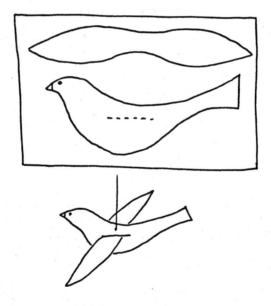

Project 3: Circle Snake

Give each child a large construction paper circle to color and decorate. Then use a black felt-tipped pen and trace an even spiral (each line about an inch apart). Children cut along the spiral line until they have a snake.

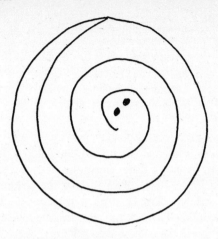

Project 4: Paper Bag Puppets

Use lunch bags. Glue a circle cut slightly larger than the square bottom of the bag. This circle becomes the face. Give children yarn for hair, buttons for eyes, colored paper scraps, and wallpaper to decorate. Then they can put a hand in the puppet and move the face part up and down. You can do a similar project with old white socks to make sock puppets.

Project 5: Puppet Theater

Use a large box with an opening cut in the front for the stage. Allow children to paint and decorate (this is a good outdoor sunny day project). Attach fabric across the top for a curtain. Encourage children to make puppet shows, take turns being the audience, make tickets, and so on.

Project 6: Mother's Day Poster

First make copies of this little poem:

> Sometimes you get discouraged,
> Because I am so small
> And I always leave my fingerprints
> On windows, doors, and wall
> But every day I'm growing
> I'll be grown-up someday

And all those tiny fingerprints
Will surely fade away
So here's one final handprint
Just so you can recall
Exactly how my fingers looked
When I was very small

When you make copies of this poem, set it off to one side to allow room for a handprint. Then have the children dip their right hands into paint (bright or dark colors work best) and carefully press onto this paper. It is a nice touch to have the children write their names in a matching color. Then you can mount the paper on the same color poster board to create an attractive and touching memento. (Do not forget to put the date on the back.)

Project 7: Mother's Day Stationery

Make potato prints in the shapes of flowers (about 2″ wide). Allow children to stamp one or two flower prints in each corner of blank typing paper and on the front of an envelope (lower left corner). Use pastel-colored paints in meat trays. After paint is dry, children can use green felt-tipped pens to make stems and leaves on the flower. You can also use wallpaper to make folders to contain the stationery and stamp flowers on the front.

Project 8: Giant Flowers

Use paper plates and paint to create big flowers. One plate is for the flower head, and the other can be cut as shown to create the leaves and stem. These make fun decorations to brighten up a room. (See diagram.)

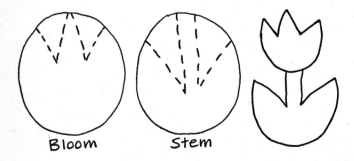

Bloom   Stem

Project 9: Pressed Flower Pictures

Plan a walk where children can pick wildflowers. Even an empty lot might have some. Bring the flowers home and press them between sheets of wax paper and heavy books. Leave for a couple of days. Then carefully remove (leaving them between the wax paper). Gently iron wax paper (with regular paper between wax paper and surface of iron). Trim the edges of wax paper and create a frame by folding lengthwise strips of construction paper to staple around the edges of the wax paper. You can punch a hole on the two top corners and thread a piece of yarn through to make a hanger. (These also make nice Mother's Day gifts.)

Project 10: Memorial Day Flags

First draw a flag design onto 8″ x 11″ paper, and make enough copies to have one for each child. Then provide 1½″ squares of red, white, and blue tissue paper. Display a real flag for children to look at as they squinch tissue paper and glue onto their own papers to create collage flags.

Other Projects and Ideas

Summer Projects: Picnics. Walks. Nature hikes. Water play. Sidewalk chalk drawing. Puppet shows. Berry picking. Bug watching. Outdoor art. Finger painting. Mural painting.

Some Ideas for Weekly Themes: Jungle Week. Farmer Week. Pioneer Week. Ocean Week. Desert Week. Forest Week. International Week.

How to Incorporate a Theme for Circus Week: Make circus posters. Have lawn acrobats with circus music and tightrope (balance beam) walkers. Have a Wild (Stuffed) Animal Day. Organize a marching circus band. Have a Clown Day with face paint and fun!

Shoe Day: Ask children to bring old canvas tennis shoes, and allow them to decorate them by gluing on buttons, lace, or sequins or using fabric paint.

Tie-Dye: Ask children to bring a white T-shirt, and use rubber bands to twist and tie with strings. Dye them all together.

Friendship Bracelets: (For five-year-olds and up; younger ones will need help.) Tie four 12″ strands of bright colored yarn to a large safety pin. Tell children to pin this to a pant leg so they can use the leg as a table. You make a four-strand braid by separating two strands to each side, then take the farthest strand from the outside and place it in the center. Then take one from the other farthest side and place it in the center. Keep taking the strands from the outside into the center, alternating sides each time. You will end up with a flat braid. Children love making these into bracelets and exchanging them with friends. You can do the same thing with six, eight, or ten strands (but the more strands you use, the lighter weight the yarn or string should be).

About the Author

Even though Melody Carlson moved from providing child-care as a business, she cannot seem to leave children behind, in her heart or in her life. Her current job is with Holt International Children's Services, an international adoption agency that places homeless children from all around the world with U.S. families.

Melody continues to write, and may someday make that into her next home business, but for now she finds much fulfillment in work. Her boys are both teenagers, and the family finally built her husband's dream house (designed by Melody!) in Springfield, Oregon. The Carlsons' goal, as a family, is to enjoy the teen era before the boys go off to college. They recently bought a little ski boat, and look forward to some good family times on the lake.